A selection from
the 2010 J.P. Morgan
Holiday Reading List

With best wishes for

The Wallace Family

J.P.Morgan
J.P. Morgan Securities

GREEN LIVING

ARCHITECTURE AND PLANNING

GREEN LIVING

ARCHITECTURE AND PLANNING

THE PRINCE'S FOUNDATION
FOR THE BUILT ENVIRONMENT

RIZZOLI
NEW YORK

New York · Paris · London · Milan

The Prince's Foundation
FOR THE BUILT ENVIRONMENT

First published in the United States of America in 2010 by
Rizzoli International Publications, Inc.
300 Park Avenue South
New York, NY 10010

www.rizzoliusa.com

Originally published in the United Kingdom as *Tradition &
Sustainability* in 2010 by Compendium Publishing Limited
43 Frith Street, London W1D 4SA

www.compendiumpublishing.com

2010 2011 2012 2013 / 10 9 8 7 6 5 4 3 2 1

ISBN: 978-0-8478-3310-8

Library of Congress Control Number: 2009936371

Design: John Shuttleworth

Draftsman: Mark Franklin

Printed in China through Printworks Int. Ltd.

Acknowledgments

The Prince's Foundation for the Built Environment should like to
thank the following for their assistance with the project: Dr. Barbara
Kenda for the initial work on commissioning and packaging the
material; Steven Parissien; Richard Hayward; editors Gloria Ohland
and Kateri Butler; Jo St. Mart for photo research; and, of course, the
authors, without whose contributions there would be no book.

Pages 2 and 5: *A New
Campus for the American
University in Cairo: the
master plan by Dr. Abdel
Halim I. Abdel Halim. It is
a tangible symbol for the
durability of traditional
knowledge in dealing with a
wide variety of environmental
challenges in both the urban
context and its individual
architectural equivalent.*

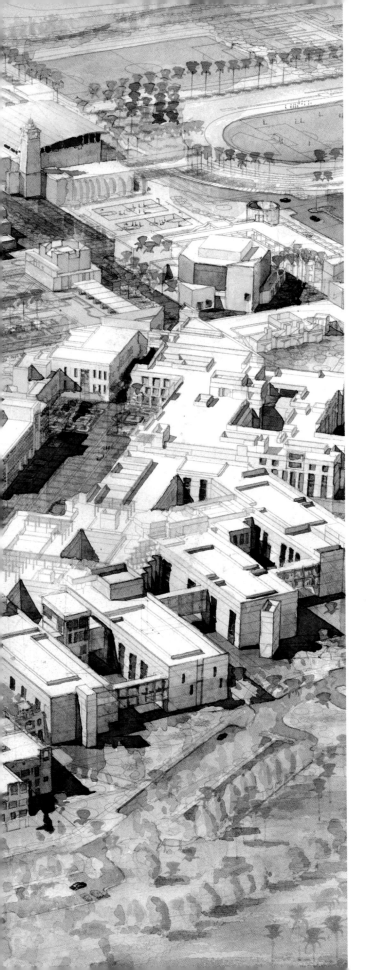

Contents

CLARENCE HOUSE

This collection of essays is, perhaps, a useful corrective to the assumption that environmental buildings need be primarily led by technological innovation. The authors have each contributed a specialist perspective to a general theme; that the act of building was historically – and could be again – the development of a living tradition, in which accumulated knowledge meant successive generations of builders learnt from what had gone before and buildings were the embodiment of accumulated wisdom. The principle holds true for both buildings and neighbourhood planning, and has guided the work of my Foundation for the Built Environment in the design of new communities to reflect the aspirations of ordinary people.

These neighbourhoods have daily needs – schools and local shops – at their heart, are of discernable and attractive character and, furthermore, accrue higher value over time than the standard housing estate. Recently, my Foundation has built a prototype low energy dwelling – The Natural House, represented in this book – that seeks to demonstrate how the best lessons of tradition can be embodied in an "Eco-Vernacular" with a projected life of 200 years rather than 25. This, to me, is a true understanding of "sustainability".

Other interpretations of "sustainable design" have seen the appearance of homes dictated by the operational requirements of photovoltaics, wind turbines, solar traps and the other trappings of environmental science. This approach excludes a more holistic response to energy performance, one understood by previous generations of vernacular builders. In this tradition energy was not wasted, simply because it was so hard to come by. Before the age of plentiful energy cheapened architecture, windows were proportioned to let light deep into rooms, walls were of sufficient thickness to capture heat within rooms on Winter nights, but keep out the sun on hot days, and building materials were, by circumstance, of local provenance and chosen for longevity.

"Sustainability" is not laboratory science; it is a principle manifest in the legacy of historic buildings all around us. We now see professional designers and planners acknowledging the folly in construction practice in the late twentieth century. "Lay" opinion, on the other hand, has for many years demanded the preservation and enhancement of historic areas and individual buildings; their qualities of beauty and local distinctiveness becoming their defence against obliteration. As with the plight of the polar bear and other rare wildlife, the best defence mechanism of our historic environment in the face of threat is a universally recognized beauty. This is not a subjective quality – natural beauty has a base in the awe-inspiring logic of natural law and Nature's fundamental power over anything humans may set out to achieve.

I look forward to a future in which we are mature enough to see how we are not apart from Nature, but part of her pattern and subject to her rules. When we do this – and I pray it is sooner rather than later, for the clock is ticking inexorably towards catastrophe – we will see how we have both a debt and a duty to conserving natural resources that go beyond the carbon challenge to address overpopulation, food and farming and the allocation of resources between competing interests, both locally and internationally. At this scale of comprehension the rules for an Eco-Vernacular in building will seem obvious, moving from targets for heat loss and electricity consumption to a much broader picture of low energy communities that are places people want to build, to be in and in which they take collective pride.

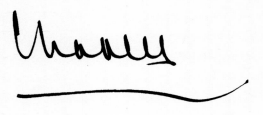

HRH the Prince of Wales visits the Natural House at the UK Building Research Establishment, designed by the Prince's Foundation for the Built Environment to demonstrate the environmental performance of natural materials, May 19, 2009.

Sustainability and Tradition:

Two Sides of the Coin

Hank Dittmar

" The Brundtland Commission's definition of sustainable development, embraces the notion of limiting growth to the use of natural and human capital, and introduces the notion of rootedness in place, habitat, and culture. Perhaps most importantly, it restores to the idea of sustainability the link idea that we can learn from past generations as well as from present technology. "

Sustainability has come to be associated with cutting-edge technology, and in architecture, with glass, steel, solar panels, and wind turbines. Most images of proposed eco cities feature moody art direction inspired by the film *Blade Runner*, and buildings derived from the high-tech modernism of the two British architectural lords, Richard Rogers and Norman Foster. In fact, a recent study found that 79 percent of Britons surveyed viewed sustainable housing as being associated with the term *high tech* and over 90 percent viewed sustainable housing as "modern" rather than "old-fashioned."[1] Americans overwhelmingly look to technology for sustainability as well, with the Harris Poll finding that 67 percent of those surveyed favored technology applications to produce "green products and services."[2]

A second, smaller strand of thought views sustainability as being associated with the "less-is-more," "back-to-the-land" movements of the sixties and seventies. This "hobbit green," as opposed to "high-tech green," features homes called "earth ships," made of tires and built largely underground, and a do-it-yourself aesthetic. A small but growing movement for co-housing—jointly owned housing developments with shared kitchens and common areas—in the United States exemplifies this trend. In the United Kingdom, the Transition Town movement, championed by Rob Hopkins and pioneered by the town of Totnes, looks to a local economy, local

money, and a dramatically reduced ecological footprint through voluntary local association.

The problem with both the high-tech vision and with hobbit green is that by and large consumers want to live in a traditional house with modern conveniences in a traditional setting and work in a traditional office building. Surveys in both the U.S. and the U.K. typically show that a large majority of consumers prefer to live in traditional homes.[3] If the only routes to sustainability are the Buck Rogers and the hobbit routes, then consumers will find themselves left out.

Clearly, if sustainability and high-technology style are viewed as linked in the eyes of consumers, and consumers prefer traditional settings, it will be harder to get them to adopt sustainable practices in the built environment. At the same time, tradition is viewed with scorn among built-environment professionals, derided as kitsch and as pastiche, resulting in a disconnect between the professionals and their clients. As T. S. Eliot remarked of tradition in 1922, "seldom does the word appear except in a phrase of censure. If otherwise, it is vaguely approbative, with the implication . . . of some pleasing archaeological reconstruction."[4]

If, as this book amply demonstrates, tradition and the vernacular have much to teach us about sustainability, and in fact can serve as the base from which to evolve cities, towns, and buildings that can respond to our global environmental challenges, then resolving this seeming conflict is as much a matter of better social marketing as anything else. Perhaps the answers have been right under our noses the whole time, if we look past the last fifty years of planning and architectural trends to the deeper patterns that have provided the foundation for human settlement on the planet for more than a few thousand years.

Resolving this conflict will require better definitions of both sustainability and tradition, and the reestablishment of living traditions that evolve to confront contemporary challenges.

On Sustainability

> Sustainable development is development that meets the needs of the present without compromising the ability of future generations to meet their own needs.—"Our Common Future: Report of the World Commission on Environment and Development," 1987.[5]

In defining sustainability, it is useful to go right back to the origins of the term, with the United Nations Brundtland Commission in 1987. The commission was charged with reconciling the challenge of a developing world with the natural environment, and their definition (above) clearly placed sustainability in an intergenerational and global context. The challenges of the present day must be resolved in a way that does not reduce choices for future generations. The Brundtland Commission recognized two key concepts: the notion that there must be limits in the present day, and the notion that a global commons extends to future generations as well.

Since the 1987 report, the notion of sustainability has been widely embraced, and has been viewed as having three interrelated components: environment, equity, and economy. This three-pronged approach was taken up in the U.S. by the President's Council on Sustainable Development, an initiative of the Clinton Administration championed by then Vice President Al Gore. Each of the three sectors has since argued that their sector is most important, and that it is getting short shrift, and as a result the core notion of a compact between generations has tended to be lost.

At the same time, this has lead to a concept of sustainability as being essentially the domain of technical people, who will manage a set of inputs and outputs on a global scale balancing the three sectors in a sort of big black box. This concept can be contrasted to the ecological approach to sustainability, which sees it as being rooted in culture and adaptation to place. This notion of a human ecology of sustainability was developed by David Orr in his book *The Nature of Design*:

> Settled cultures, without using the word "ecology," have designed with ecology in mind because to do otherwise would bring ruin, famine and social disintegration. Out of necessity they created harmony between intentions and the genius of particular places that preserved diversity of both natural and biological capital; utilized current solar income, created little or no waste, imposed few unaccounted costs and supported cultural and social patterns.[6]

This notion of an ecological approach to design incorporates the intergenerational idea of linking present with future embodied in the Brundtland Commission's definition of sustainable development, embraces the notion of limiting growth to the use of natural and human capital, and introduces the notion of rootedness in place, habitat, and culture. Perhaps most importantly, it restores to the idea of sustainability the link idea that we can learn from past generations as well as from present technology. This brings us to the idea of tradition.

On Tradition

> Yet if the only form of tradition, of handing down, consisted in following the ways of the immediate generation before us in a blind or timid adherence to its successes, "tradition" should positively be discouraged. . . . This historical sense, which is a sense of the timeless as well as of the temporal and of the timeless and of the temporal together, is what makes a writer traditional.
>
> —T. S. Eliot, "Tradition and the Individual Talent"

Traditional thinking is often derided as romanticism, and as historicism, largely because of the influence of the modern movement. History is seen as a succession of movements, with the Enlightenment and the Industrial Revolution having been succeeded in the twentieth century by the modern movement. In the arts, architecture, and in philosophy, a foundational belief of the modern movement is the idea of a "courageous break with the past, and . . . the machine-age in all its implications: new materials, new processes, new forms, new problems."[7] Architects such as Le Corbusier defined the city and the building as "machines for living," and called for "a concord between men and machines."[8]

The idea that the past was irrelevant to modern problems has become ingrained in teaching, especially in schools of architecture, and tradition and vernacular have become objects of historical study, rather than representing living processes. The rejection of tradition was linked to the creation of a series of new, technology-driven building processes, all propelled by the idea of a machine age based on fossil fuels and industrial production systems: freeways and motorways, the separation of city circulation into motorized and pedestrian zones, single-use zoning of the city into housing districts, shopping centers, office and business parks, and leisure zones, suburban tract housing, the curtain wall and the balloon frame, and a host of other innovations. The failure of many of these untested planning and design ideas is not surprising, nor is their inability to evolve to confront new ecological realities such as higher fuel prices or climate change.

In the meantime, traditional neighborhoods, streets, and buildings have quietly continued to evolve and go through cycles of decay, renewal, and rebirth as the long-term value of long-lived places continues to endure. In a study for the Prince's Foundation and the British Property Federation, the consulting firm Savills studied three conventional suburban developments, three "new urban" developments, and three historic neighborhoods, in similar market areas. The conventional projects displayed the lowest appreciation in prices over time, the "new urban" developments the second best performance, and in every case the historic neighborhoods displayed the greatest price appreciation.[9]

Webster's Dictionary describes tradition as "a long established custom or practice." Surely part of the problem in architecture and planning is that the modern movement has disrupted the custom and practice of tradition, by decreeing the past to be irrelevant. At least three generations of architects and planners have graduated from school without studying traditional architecture or urban design as a living practice, and this means that living traditional architects and urban planners are either self-taught or learned through informal apprenticeship. The situation in traditional building crafts is hardly better, with schools of traditional building only lately being established in Charleston and in the U.K. There are no university architecture schools that teach traditional architecture in the United Kingdom, and only a few that tolerate students who are

" The rejection of tradition was linked to the creation of a series of new, technology-driven building processes, all propelled by the idea of a machine age based on fossil fuels and industrial production systems."

interested in the subject. The situation is better in the United States, where at least three schools are dedicated to traditional architecture and urbanism, and a number teach it as part of a balanced architectural education.

Traditional architecture and urbanism are alive and well, however, in cities, towns, and villages across the world, and the close study of successful precedents has been a fruitful way of learning to make new places that also work. Both the American new urbanists and the British traditional urbanists have built a large body of evidence from the documentation of typologies of streets, squares, blocks, and buildings, and have gradually learned to apply the principles learned from this study to make new places that go beyond the copying of historic styles. At both the scale of the city and the scale of the building, the challenge is now one of evolving tradition to confront new challenges, including the rapid pace of development in a post-industrial urbanizing world.

Sustainable (and Traditional) Urbanism

The environmental tradition has historically been about embracing and preserving the natural places, and environmentalists have often viewed cities as dirty, polluting, unfortunate blights. This tendency to place nature and man in opposition derives from both the popular rejection of the Victorian city and its polluting factories and foul sewers, and from the roots of environmentalism in saving threatened species and preserving habitat and scenic beauty. Environmentalists responded by regulating industrial and urban discharge into water and air, through planning laws to preserve countryside and reclaim industrial land, and through preserving and conserving farmland and wild places as "green lungs" for the planet. At the same time, however, the huge growth in global population, and the move from subsistence and market farming to industrial agriculture have together brought about an urban explosion, and

cities have become a dominant feature in both the human and natural environment.

A few facts will help to make the needed connections. Despite its self-image as a nation of villagers, the United Kingdom's population is over-whelmingly urban, with 90 percent living in urban places, according to the United Nations. The population of the United States is similarly concentrated in metropolitan areas. In 2007, the earth officially became an urban planet, with over half of the world's population living in cities. Globally, the twenty-first century will be the urban century. According to the United Nations Environment Programme, of the global population increase of 2.2 billion by 2030, 2.1 billion will live in urban areas, and by 2030, over more than 60 percent of the world's population will be urban dwellers.[10]

Two issues arise here: First, if all these urban dwellers adopt the suburban living patterns and lifestyles of the United States and Western Europe, the climate problem will be greatly exacerbated. Second, many if not most of the new urban dwellers in the Southern Hemisphere live in grossly overcrowded slums, rife with cholera and other diseases, and where infant mortality, malnutrition, and lack of secure land tenure are endemic problems. These slums may be environmentally sustainable, but only because their residents have next to nothing.

Global urbanization is thus both a social and environmental issue, and the challenge of raising global living standards while reducing carbon emissions is a knotty problem. By and large, then, this trend toward global urbanization is seen as a problem worldwide—for all of the traditional reasons about pollution and overcrowding, plus challenges of public health, nutrition, and engagement in civil society.

People all over the world are moving to cities for a reason, and that reason is that cities are seen as offering

"In 2007, the earth officially became an urban planet, with over half of the world's population living in cities."

the opportunity for a better life: because they provide the chance for employment, training, and access to health care, to education, and to the online world. In other words, cities are efficient places for humans, and increasingly are key to a successful human ecology. For when we look at urban places, we find not only solutions to the personal transport part of the climate problem—density, connected streets, accessible public transport, more efficient buildings, and mixed use—but also solutions for the broader social challenge of truly sustainable development.

Thinking of cities as habitat for humans (and songbirds, insects, and small mammals!) means organizing cities in ways that offer different choices in our day-to-day lives: greener ways of living, of moving around—or not having to move around so much—of delivering food and services. Responding to the urgent crises of climate change is often seen as a burden, and as a threat. People fear that life in the future will be more

limited, and that being green means making sacrifices. That's not necessarily so: the shift to green, resource-efficient cities could well add to quality of life, and in fact people might eat better, be healthier, and have just as many choices as before. They will just be different choices!

The fundamental premise is that thinking of cities as artifacts of natural processes might inform the way we plan and design. Cities might be planned to evolve organically, rather than in a mechanical fashion. What are the implications of such an approach for the quality of people's lives?

First, we might begin by defining the properties of healthy ecosystems, and look to apply those properties to the conscious process of city-making. A series of attributes emerges from the study of complex systems: basic typologies that change slowly, but are highly flexible and adaptable, built-in redundancy as a way of ensuring reliability, and feedback loops as a way of responding to change. Anthropologist and systems theorist Gregory Bateson called for "a single system of environment combined with high human civilization, in which the flexibility of the civilization shall match that of the environment to create an ongoing complex system, open-ended for slow change of even basic characteristics."[11]

The notion that cities are composed, like eco-systems, of basic types, which change slowly, but are flexible and adaptable, is being applied in the Foundation's work in town planning for historic town centers. In his book *How Buildings Learn*, American author and deep-green thinker Stewart Brand introduced the concept of "pace layering," meaning that different parts of a building—or a city—change at different rates.[12] The slow layers are meant to be most adaptable and longest-lived, while the fast layers respond and change quickly. As you can see from my adaptation of Stewart Brand's diagram of rates of change (Figure 1), nature is a fundamental layer of civilization, meant to change most

Figure 1: *Rates of change in cities.*

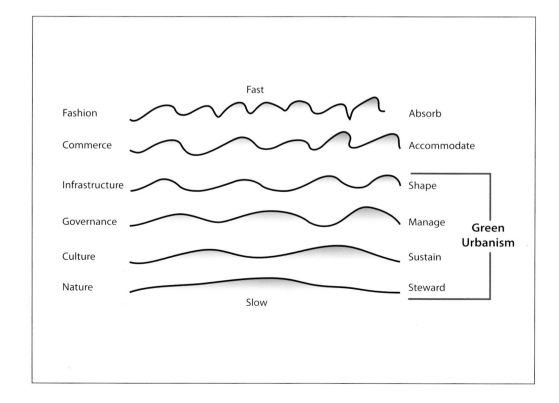

slowly, while fashion skims the surface, changing by vagary and whim. When this idea is adapted to city planning, we begin to develop a new sense of priorities, acting as steward for nature, and accommodating short-term trends like retail formats and commerce within the flexible fabric of the urban structure rather than altering fundamental structures to adjust to them.

Scale means understanding the role of buildings, streets, neighborhoods, towns, and regions in a complex system. Regions are about the interaction of complex systems: markets, the institutions that regulate them, and the transport that creates access to them. Regions are made up of a system of walkable neighborhoods, interconnected by streets and transport networks, each serving its own function.

Scale makes it possible to operate public transport systems efficiently, providing a meaningful alternative to the automobile. Scale also allows the provision of environmental infrastructure such as sustainable urban drainage or combined heat and power that are more cost effective at the neighborhood or district level.

An interconnected street network provides for a better distribution of traffic, lessening congestion on major roads. The avoidance of "wiggly worm" cul-de-sacs allows for the creation of walkable neighborhoods that accommodate the automobile but celebrate the pedestrian.

A mixed community is built around the form of streets, blocks, and buildings, and the types of buildings rather than type of land use. It allows for employment and retail to be close to residences. Mixed communities also provide a range of housing types and sizes, accommodating affordable housing through "pepper potting" rather than in monocultural disconnected estates.

These characteristics add up to something called location efficiency. Location efficiency, which can be quantified, is the combination of greater residential density, increased pedestrian and bicycle friendliness, and access to public transport. Improved location efficiency results in reduced vehicle travel, lower carbon emissions, and reduced household transportation expenses.

If we look at cities and towns in terms of per capita environmental burden, rather than on an area-wide basis, they are far more environmentally friendly than sprawling suburbs. On a per-square-mile basis, city centers seem far dirtier than the suburbs and farmland, because of the concentration of roads and cars and buildings. But when one recalculates on a per capita basis, a very different story emerges: on a per capita basis, city centers contribute much less carbon than do suburban areas. The combination of scale, density, street connectivity, and mixed community makes all the difference.

Figure 2 shows the impact in the San Francisco Bay Area. It demonstrates the effect of residential household travel, based on a massive study I helped to lead on the travel of millions of households in the metropolitan areas

Figure 2: *Cities and CO_2: Carbon emissions in the San Francisco Bay area, depicted on a per square mile basis and on a per capita basis.*

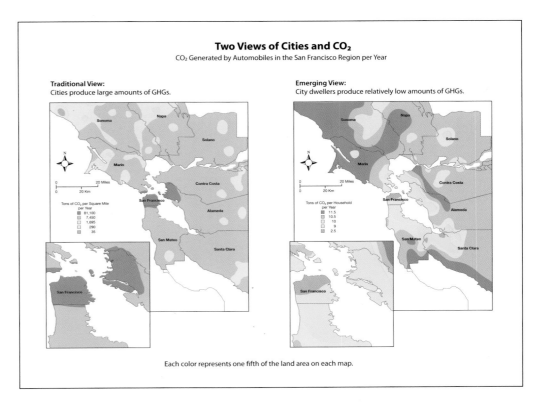

13

of Chicago, Southern California, and the San Francisco Bay Area. As one can see, the impact is profound and consistent across the region, with a doubling of density leading to a halving of vehicle travel. Figure 3 depicts the same relationships in London, based upon work done by the Prince's Foundation for the Built Environment for the London Borough of Waltham Forest and the London Development Authority.

In this project, the Prince's Foundation for the Built Environment, with partners including the Center for Neighborhood Technology, Space Syntax, and Seth Harry Associates, undertook a master plan for the highly accessible London suburban town center of Walthamstow, seeking to increase the stock of affordable housing, improve accessibility, safety, and the retail offer, and at the same time reduce per capita carbon

emissions. Through a unique participatory design process called Enquiry by Design, the Foundation worked with local authorities, residents, and businesses to create a master plan that preserved existing neighborhood character with the addition of mid-rise mixed-use development based on historic building types, improved walkable access to the town center and public transport, and proposed the reorientation of public transport routes in the center.

The resulting plan accommodated over 2,400 new residences while reducing carbon emissions from vehicle travel by three tons per household per annum. It was supported by two-thirds of residents surveyed and has been adopted by the London Borough of Waltham Forest.[13] The combination of a grounding in traditional urban patterns and building typologies, engagement with

Figure 3: *CO$_2$ emissions from motor vehicles per household in greater London.*

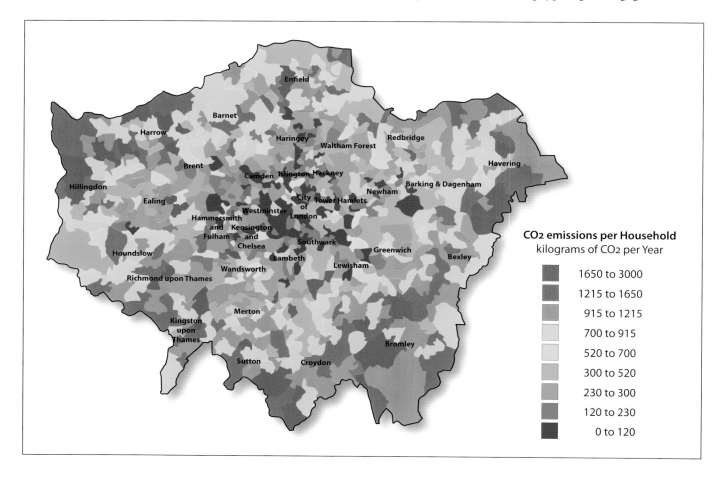

community in order to tap into local intelligence, and the use of evidence-based tools like the location efficiency model and space syntax methodology move the Walthamstow project from traditional urbanism to sustainable urbanism.

Residential densities allowing for exchange, interconnected street patterns, public transport systems, and mixed use are characteristics of traditional urban communities, and properly designing for sustainability means being grounded in an ever-evolving tradition. Figure 4 contrasts the development pattern of late-twentieth-century suburban sprawl with sustainable (and traditional) urbanism. If one views tradition rather than self-conscious newness as a foundation for sustainability, then the challenge is one of reconnecting with adaptation to place, and employing new evidence-based tools for evolving applicable precedents to confront and solve new challenges.

Two examples of this approach come from the Prince's Foundation's master-planning work at Lincoln and at Upton in Northamptonshire.

Continuity and Context in Lincoln

Lincoln, where the Prince's Foundation was asked to develop a new master plan for the city center, is very different from the essentially Victorian London suburb of Walthamstow. The Romans founded the city more than two thousand years ago, and the challenge at Lincoln is to find a way to repair the damage to its physical environment, accessibility, and sense of community from the past century of industrialization, motorization, and inward-facing shopping centers.

Stewart Brand's thinking about rates of change and the diagram presented earlier in cities helped us at Lincoln, providing a sustainability tool for unpicking the changes over time. The diagram places the work of the master planner in the context of nature, culture, governance, infrastructure, commerce, and fashion.

With nature the role of the planner is one of stewardship, and with culture one of sustaining, rather than a more active role. The master planner stands in for governance in this case, mediating the need to maintain and husband cultural and ecological resources against the demands of the present; for infrastructure, which has shaped communities; for commerce, which must be accommodated; and for fashion, the fastest changing—think about window displays or mobile-phone stores—which should be absorbed.

When we looked at Lincoln during our workshops, we found that this was certainly the case, as the city center had been altered dramatically in the past century and a half. First came the introduction of the railway at grade, severing the city center from neighborhoods to the south. Second came the imposition of grade-separated road systems, creating further barriers, especially to the east and west. Recent developments of

Figure 4: *The development pattern of late-twentieth-century suburban sprawl contrasted with sustainable urbanism.*

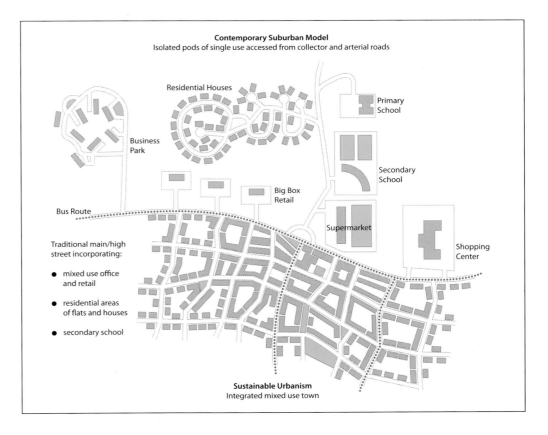

both government buildings and shopping centers have altered the basic structure of streets and pedestrian movement, walling off the river, hampering movement across the city, and destroying continuity with a rich building tradition.

As all of these interventions reach the end of their useful life, the opportunity emerges to create an enduring framework for shaping the town center that restores the ability to adapt flexibly to change while respecting the legacy of this ancient city. At its core, the town-center strategy for Lincoln, which emerged from intensive research and engagement with stakeholders, consists of a series of interventions in the transportation network and at key places in the city center. When accomplished over a multiyear time frame, these interventions will restore the basic circulatory system that gives life to the city and access to services, amenities, and opportunity for its inhabitants, and sets out a stable framework of building and road types that will enable the city of Lincoln to adapt and remain a principal urban center for the Eastern Midlands into the foreseeable future.

Most importantly, the framework plan replaces the governing notion of planning intervention in the modern era—difference, and a conscious break with the past—with a new theme of continuity with the built and natural legacy of the great cathedral city of Lincoln. A city that has endured for almost two thousand years ought to be planned so that it can continue to endure, and even to thrive. If a robust partnership can hold and champion this plan over that time, the result will be a city that can once again learn from its past, and apply those lessons to enable it to thrive and sustain into the future. The idea of continuity runs contrary to current preservation dogma, which stresses difference and distinction—"the honestly modern"—but aligns closely with both common sense and thousands of years of building tradition.

" Centuries of vernacular and traditional building have much to teach us about how to live within our limits. "

Sustainable Drainage at Upton, Northamptonshire

A major problem with twentieth-century urban and suburban development has been the way that it has dealt with storm water and drainage through channelization and underground pipes and culverts. This engineering approach to drainage has tended to create downstream flooding problems and water-quality problems, and it has reduced the ability of aquifers to recharge naturally. As a result, in recent years engineers have begun to try to evolve sustainable urban drainage techniques that reduce the amount of impervious surfaces in new development and attempt to handle storm water on site through infiltration into ground water and through detention basins that delay discharge into stream systems. The engineering solutions have been intended solely to deal with stormwater issues, and when imposed upon urban plans, tend to break up the pattern of walkable blocks, create large "no-go" areas, and impose large concrete structures upon roadsides and residential neighborhoods—a typical result of single-order solutions that do not deal with the complexity of urban environments.

At Upton in Northamptonshire, where the Prince's Foundation and EDAW worked with the local borough and English Partnerships to master plan an urban extension to the town of five thousand residences, flooding downstream in the River Nene was always a key issue. As a result, sustainable drainage was integrated into the scheme from the outset, with the goal of doing so in a way that worked well with the creation of walkable, human-scaled streets and a pleasant green network of public spaces. The sustainable drainage swales were integrated into the street sections in a way that is properly enclosed and well landscaped, making a scenic virtue of a sustainability necessity. The photograph on page 17 depicts one of the streets that was built as a result of the master plan.

The Foundation has taken the idea further at Romsey in Hampshire, looking into traditional ways of

Left: *Sustainable urban drainage and traditional urbanism in Upton, Northamptonshire.*

Marsh	Stream	Canaletto	Shallow Street Gutter
Retention Pond	Brook	Ditch	Outlet

Figure 5: *A range of sustainable drainage solutions in Romsey, Hampshire.*

handling water in these ancient towns and villages to derive sustainable drainage solutions that reflect local adaptation and culture. Figure 5 depicts a range of sustainable drainage solutions that are being applied in two new developments at Romsey, all of them equally grounded in traditional urbanism and the latest flood guidance from the U.K. Environment Agency.

In all of these examples, the Foundation employs a three-stage design process, beginning with a grounding in traditional urbanism, seeking to understand how it has been adapted in a place through time and response to local conditions, economy, and geography, and then

evolving it using a series of evidence-based design tools to refine the developing master plan. The Foundation does all of this in situ, utilizing the Enquiry by Design methodology to engage expert stakeholders in an inter-disciplinary inquiry, tap into community concerns and local intelligence, and move between scales to consider the whole along with the parts.

Sustainable (and Traditional) Buildings

At the scale of the city, the town, and the neighborhood, it is clear that traditional urbanism can be demonstrated to have profound sustainability implications, and that the process of evolving traditional urban patterns to confront today's sustainability challenges is well under way. Just as clearly, centuries of vernacular and traditional building have much to teach us about how to live within our limits, but does tradition provide a platform for dealing with the very real problems of rapid global urbanization?

First, sustainability means building for the long term—one hundred years, rather than twenty years. Sustainability, as the Brundtland Commission defined it, is about making choices today that preserve choices for future generations—and that is also about creating a link with the past by understanding what tradition has to teach us, adapting it for present needs to make something that will be successful in a hundred years.

Second, because of this need for long-term thinking, it is essential to build in an adaptable, flexible, and resilient manner, reassessing and reusing existing buildings wherever possible and making new buildings and neighborhoods that can learn, in the words of Stewart Brand, "The immediate program is not the generator, as the building should be designed to evolve, changing use over time as the user and the city around it may require."[14]

Third, building in a manner that fits the place, in terms of materials used, proportion and layout, and climate, ecology, and building practices. Instead of architecture as a global brand, what's needed is globalism from the bottom up, a design practice that enables local places to compete globally on the basis of distinctive character, local identity, and place.

Fourth, building beautifully, in a manner that builds upon tradition, evolving it in response to present challenges and utilizing the best and most appropriate new technologies and techniques. Beautiful buildings can be defined simply, as buildings that are loved, and because they are loved, they will be cared for, be renewed, and be sustainable as a result.

Fifth, understanding the purpose of a building or group of buildings within the hierarchy of the buildings around it and responding with an appropriate building type and design. Doing this often implies composition of a harmonious whole, rather than the erection of singular objects of architectural or corporate will. In the city, most buildings are background buildings that stand as part of a composition, not singular objects, and could draw their character more from their neighbors than from the singular vision of the designer or client.

And finally, understanding that the role of the designer in this world crisis is less an act of creation and more the craft of marrying skills with local intelligence through community engagement, deep understanding of local identity and character, and the knowledge that most of the time what is required are background buildings.

An explication of the Foundation's work in natural low-carbon buildings is provided in the chapter by James Hulme. But it is worth noting that all of our work in sustainable architecture is grounded in a sustainability process that begins with the application of a set of general principles (those outlined above), and proceeds to a deep study examination of local precedent and adaptation both through study on the ground and engagement with local communities, and then to a review of key challenges and the assessment and integration of appropriate new technologies, materials, and tools. In this way sustainability and tradition are evolved in a manner that both resonates with culture and place and takes it forward into the future.

Beyond "Ism"

His Royal Highness The Prince of Wales, founder of the Prince's Foundation for the Built Environment and, more recently, the Prince's Rainforest Project, has campaigned for decades on sustainability issues. He received the Vincent Scully Prize from the U.S. National Building

" Traditional urbanism can be demonstrated to have profound sustainability implications, and . . . the process of evolving traditional urban patterns to confront today's sustainability challenges is well under way. "

Museum for his contribution to architectural and urban practice, theory, and criticism. In his acceptance speech, he called for a union of tradition and modernity, beyond the tyranny of "traditionalism" or "modernism":

To find new solutions for these major global issues it is essential that we combine a thorough under- standing of how past civilizations ordered them- selves, using minimal resources, together with new science and technologies so that we really can have our "cake and eat it." Modernism has led us to seek answers in a host of technical "fixes." Tradition- alism often only pays it lip service. Real traditional thinking has always tried to see the whole picture.[15]

Below: *Illustration of canaletto block in master plan for sustainable urban extension in Romsey, Hampshire.*

Above: *R. Buckminster Fuller, architect and inventor of the geodesic dome.*

Left: *The Montreal Biosphère Environment Museum, designed by Buckminster Fuller, is dedicated to water and the environment.*

Right: *Interior of the Pantheon, Rome, A.D. 180. The Romans and many other great pre-industrial civilizations built extremely well without fossil fuels. In some ways their work was superior to the structures routinely erected today: a modern engineering firm hired to design a Pantheon would not produce a structure able to last two thousand years. What did the Romans—and the Greeks, Egyptians, Indians, Persians, Mayans, Inca, and Chinese—know that we've forgotten?*

Left and Below Left: *Mesa Verde, southwestern Colorado, and the concert hall at Bard College, Annandale-on-Hudson, New York: Both of these buildings demonstrate the most sophisticated architecture and technology of their times. One is keenly adapted to its climate, staying warm in winter, cool in summer, and safe from marauders all year around. The other is a sculptural wad of metal completely dependent on fossil fuels in order to be of use or comfort to human occupants. One fits into and complements its surroundings; the other is imposed from afar onto a lush riverside landscape.*

last, but many of the successes are still with us today, either as the monuments erected by kings, pharaohs, and emperors or as the still-living architectural traditions of indigenous cultures everywhere. From the cathedral at Bath to Hagia Sophia in Istanbul to the myriad forms of earthen dwellings from five continents—ever dismissed and derided as "mud huts"—pre-industrial building shows its worth in great measure because it *lasts*. With many thousands of years of experience to draw on, people in every corner of the globe had by long before Columbus' time developed refined means of creating shelter well suited to their needs and environment.

Then, something changed.

About the middle of the eighteenth century, a deforested England was mining and burning coal to keep itself warm, but could only dig down to the top of the water table. Necessity spawned invention, and the coal-powered steam engine was soon invented and at work, pumping water from the mines. More than a few people saw that those same engines could be used for a great many purposes, and the Industrial Revolution was born. We were then very suddenly a turbocharged species with opposable thumbs, riding this gift of the gods to unimaginable new heights. We could grow food, make clothing, and build buildings like never before. We could fly, we could talk across oceans, we could walk on the moon—with everyone watching on TV! Even the nuclear and computer eras that began in the twentieth century can be seen as extensions of—and still highly dependent on—the oil-based Industrial Revolution. We were and still are like adolescent children, with our sudden access to the Internet and semiautomatic weapons, having power beyond our dreams but almost no wisdom or experience to guide our hands.

And now we are finally seeing the price tag, here at the dawn of the twenty-first century, for our historic rush of wild energy. Even as the surging population wants to enjoy the same affluence as the lucky upper few percent of the world's people, the dire effects of the oil already used are becoming painfully apparent. Billions of pounds of toxic or hazardous materials are produced annually, materials whose end forms and by-products are then discarded in our soil, air, and water. Even your body is a repository for unknown and untested chemicals, and has in it about five hundred substances that didn't even exist on the planet a century ago. We grew up throwing things away, only to find out that there really is no "away." A few substances are so highly dangerous and toxic that they will require constant vigilance and maintenance by our grandchildren and their grandchildren. Then there is the need for thousands of complex regulations to restrain the rate at which we poison each other, and the life all around us upon which we unmetaphorically depend. And there is the accelerated loss of biodiversity, with extinctions happening at ten thousand times the normal background rate (alarming because any biologist or engineer knows that complexity in a system often equals robustness and resiliency, and the ability to adapt to injury, pollution, or loss).

Moreover, the oil is running out. There was only so much to start with, so the question of the party ending is not "*If*" but merely "*How soon, and how hard?*"

It's a little bit like a story my wife told me of her youth. When she and her three siblings were teenagers, their parents left the house for a weekend away, and word spread in about an hour to every neighboring county. The party that ensued was legendary, and no one ever really knew how many kids showed up for the fun. They were basically good kids, though, or at least smart enough to clean up before Mom and Dad got home. And clean up they did, leaving (they thought) no trace. Except for two little things: six garbage cans out by the garage were now full to the brim with beer cans, and someone had thrown up, wildly, copiously, and, unbeknownst to anyone else, onto the middle of Mom and Dad's bed. Mom and Dad noticed.

We're more than a little bit like those kids, having a great time now in the confidence that we can and will properly clean up before the folks—or in this case our own children and grandchildren—come home and have to clean up for us. We're drinking all the beer and leaving a stink where we think it won't matter.

The Way of Oil: Architecture on Steroids

The way we build is very much a part of the global problem. We use gas and oil instead of good design, sun, and wind to keep our spaces comfortable. We use toxic materials in the usually mistaken belief that they will give us nicer, dryer, softer, prettier surfaces. (Often, they just make us sick. Future generations will surely look back in disbelief and compare us—and our ubiquitous use of formaldehyde-based furniture and building products—to the medieval surgeons who would treat mentally disturbed patients by drilling holes in their skulls to release the evil spirits.) We have created new building materials such as epoxy glues, Portland cement, and polyvinyl chloride that are hugely utilitarian, but hugely expensive to the environment and climate. Any chemist in the world can tell you about the many new classes of hydrocarbons we have invented, but almost none know anything about toxicology, about the effects of these substances on the human body or on ecosystems. Any engineer in the world can tell you how to design a concrete foundation or steel or wood beam, but almost none can design a building for you with anything else—even though nature uses anything and everything very effectively as structure. And any architect can tell you about the history of modernism, but very few know or care about the many brilliant building designs of indigenous

cultures that do everything a building should do entirely "off the grid." We've forgotten our roots, and we are paying the price.

Belief Gone Bad: The Myth of Modern Building

The great enemy of the truth is very often not the lie—deliberate, contrived and dishonest, but the myth—persistent, persuasive, and unrealistic. Belief in myths allows the comfort of opinion without the discomfort of thought.
—John F. Kennedy

There is no question that the Industrial Revolution brought a great many benefits, both trivial and profound, to those it has touched. We have potable water and portable DVD players, we have insulin and the Internet, we have polyisocynurate insulation and low-e super-efficient double-pane windows. And yes, in some ways we do have better buildings. We have much more

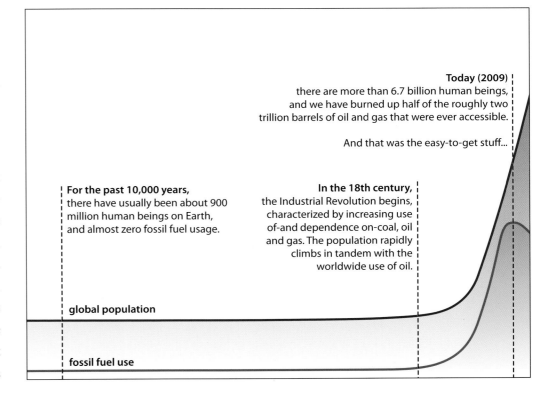

Below: Peak oil and population: You don't have to be an economist to imagine the ramifications of exponential population growth combined with falling supplies of oil and gas. No one can say with certainty when the lines may begin to diverge. It may already be happening, or it might be another fifteen or twenty years. Very few think it will be more.

Today (2009)
there are more than 6.7 billion human beings, and we have burned up half of the roughly two trillion barrels of oil and gas that were ever accessible.

And that was the easy-to-get stuff...

For the past 10,000 years, there have usually been about 900 million human beings on Earth, and almost zero fossil fuel usage.

In the 18th century, the Industrial Revolution begins, characterized by increasing use of-and dependence on-coal, oil and gas. The population rapidly climbs in tandem with the worldwide use of oil.

global population

fossil fuel use

durable, reliable roofing and waterproofing materials. Yet we also have many more moisture and mold problems because we don't skillfully use those materials. We have far better and more durable insulation, but we just don't bother to use much of it—usually just the minimum necessary to meet regulations. We have radically stronger structural materials and engineering understanding with which to make our bridges span farther, our buildings soar higher, and our public spaces vault like the sky. But we don't build for the ages, and we don't take good care of what we have.

The average person on the street probably believes we generally have much better buildings than any of our ancestors did, but with scrutiny this proves to be a myth. What we really have is a lot of cheap energy that makes up for the many flaws in our modern architecture. When that energy is no longer cheap, the buildings will no longer work very well, if at all.

We are hypnotized by the myth of the superiority of modern architecture, with the disastrous consequence of not seeing the many flaws in our work. How shall we break the spell? How shall we wake up and design and build shelter for a burgeoning world population in a way that truly makes sense—and that doesn't steal from or burden our children?

One morning on *Good Morning, Belfast!* a BBC radio talk show host asked me, "It took us thousands of years to get out of these mud huts—why would we want to get back into them?" I can't remember what I said in that moment on live radio, but I have returned to that central question many times since. It was a perfectly fair and well-phrased query, expressing as it did the common public perception—the flip side of the modernity myth—that green building or sustainability is some sort of code for "giving up the good stuff we have just finally gotten." We're not giving anything up. We're coming to our senses and returning home.

The question is: What will "returning home" mean, and how do we get from here to there? How do we give up our bad habits and use our enormous collective intelligence to create a post-industrial future? How shall we build?

Atonement and Redemption: The Rebirth of Good Building

To a very great extent, we already know how to build well—we know how to use what is at hand, rely on our personal and communal intelligence, adapt to our culture and climate, notice what works, and learn from our mistakes—but we generally just behave as if we didn't. Building well involves recovering the knowledge and experience of our ancestors, and skillfully blending that with the wealth of technical knowledge generated over the past two hundred years. It's as simple and as fabulously complex as that.

Work with the climate, not against it

Passive solar design is as old as the hills, and cultures all over the world independently figured out how to use sun and wind to control interior conditions and stave off winter's chill. The Arabs and Persians used shading, the high thermal mass of earthen walls, and prevailing breezes to keep their houses cool even in the most brutal summer heat. We have studied what they did and have begun to quantify the principles of climate-based design. Attempts to apply these principles to larger, modern buildings have had mixed results—but we do learn from each project.

Use oil well

We probably won't ever completely run out of oil; it will just become too expensive to use as casually and rapidly as we did through the twentieth century. With careful design, now known as "green chemistry," we can

Opposite: Architectural pornography: Eye-catching sculptures of steel and glass regularly get publicity and win prestigious architectural awards. But are they good buildings? They stimulate without inspiring, they dazzle but often don't function, and they usually leak. And, like pornography, people pay a great deal of money to have them; sex sells. We don't mean to single out Frank Gehry, architect of this structure, nor even the entire class of "starchitects" who dominate the public's attention. The criticism is really pointed at the starry-eyed public held in rapture, and the decision makers who consistently choose glamour over substance for the design of major buildings.

Above: *A thousand-year-old stone bridge in the Irish countryside still serves its role, even for vehicle traffic unimaginable to its builders—and it's a lovely complement to its landscape.*

Right: *A forty-year-old bridge in the U.S., built with modern engineering and modern materials, collapsed from sheer neglect.*

Opposite Above: *A two-thousand-year-old bridge built by the Romans—the Pont du Gard—soars thirty meters high and supports a canal falling a steady thirty-seven centimeters per kilometer. It is*

in every way as sophisticated as its modern counterpart, which failed disastrously after a few decades of service.

Opposite Below: *One that didn't fall down. Finally, the Rio Grande Gorge Bridge: 650 feet above the river, it was built in 1965.*

Right and Opposite:
Breaking news! Sunlight warms us up! Let the sun shine through in winter, block it in summer, and insulate well always. Good solar design is not that hard, and is a huge way to make green building far less expensive than its conventional, sun-ignoring counterpart.

perhaps continue to make use of petrochemical products—for superior insulating and waterproofing materials, for example—without creating harmful or toxic by-products.

Use what is readily available

As an examination problem, architectural and engineering students should be tasked with creating shelter, equipped with only a hunting knife, in any environment on earth. Let their imaginations take hold, but let them also be trained enough to know that precedent exists for human habitation everywhere, from the extremes of desert and arctic tundra, to the wettest tropical rainforest, to the perimeter of large urban trash dumps. (Now that more than half of humanity lives in an urban area, the scope of "natural building" can and must be extended beyond clay and natural fibers to include the detritus of industrial society.)

Straw—the new wood

Along with "mud huts," "grass shacks" have entrenched themselves in our oil mythology as emblematic of extreme poverty and wretched squalor. But over the past two decades, a growing number of architects and builders are discovering that straw fiber can in nearly every way replace wood fiber in building materials (see photographs on pages 36–37). We have precious few undisturbed forests left on earth, and comparably less high-quality timber. But we will always grow grain for our food, and will need to do something with the straw left after the harvest—there are no old-growth fields of straw to be preserved.

Build with dirt!

Everything we build with originated in the earth's crust and has its present form as a result of some combination of geological, solar, biological, and/or industrial processes. Noting that, builders need then ask how, and by what means, earth must be modified to serve any particular function in architecture. Recent developments in unstabilized earth such as adobe brick and rammed earth have clarified seismic-resistant design, moisture durability, and thermal comfort. We are for the first time in history able to build with the world's simplest material—plain earth—with great confidence about safety and performance. A well-done earthen wall is not just an acceptable substitute for its modern counterpart; it is in many important ways superior, and should be chosen whenever practicable.

Build with people!

The consensus among those thinking about a sustainable future is that everything will become more localized. Energy, food, water, textiles, and building materials will generally come from a shorter distance because it won't be worth the financial and ecological cost to toss them across the globe as we so routinely do today. Some would see that as disturbing, representing a constriction on our hard-won way of life. This author would respectfully suggest otherwise: that we will see little if any drop in quality (by almost any measure) and will rediscover our community in the process. Would you rather hire "experts" at great price to build your home, or do it yourself with your neighbors? Would you rather build with your community, involving (of course) plenty of arguments and making of mistakes, and then have good stories to tell for the rest of your lives, or would you rather "get it done" in the shortest time possible and move into a home to which you are a stranger? Possibly this is just romantic or nostalgic speculation on the part of the author—and possibly it will suddenly become the hard reality as the cost of oil rises precipitously.

" The consensus among those thinking about a sustainable future is that everything will become more localized. "

Opposite: *The container house: A very comfortable and thermally effective home was completed near Berkeley, California, by stacking used refrigerated shipping containers, adding extra insulation and finish, and building a solar atrium between. These containers are increasingly available at low cost in every city in the world—a very high-quality building material for the urban dweller.*

They're not just straw bales anymore. Industrial ecology at work: One industry's waste (the farmers' straw, **Right**) is feedstock for another industry (fiber for building materials, **Below Left and Below Right**). Waste = food. By mimicking nature, in which nothing is thrown away, we solve many problems at once. Attempts to commercialize straw panels and blocks have had a fitful start over the past two decades, but the needed technologies are now becoming clear, and structural/insulating building products are beginning to appear in the market.

Opposite: *Bales of straw are used in the construction of an otherwise traditional Cotswold cottage going up in the hills of Sonoma County. The house features rice straw bales stacked on the outside and then coated with a thick layer of plaster cement.*

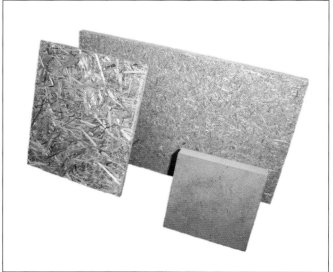

Left: *Sculptural work by Bill and Athena Steen and friends, National Museum of the American Indian, Washington, D.C., summer 2007.*

Build for the children

Reader, once I had a dream, and in this dream a spirit spoke to me:

She squinted into the afternoon sun, watching the sea fog drift through the coastal hills, and said, "What you call 'the economy' is but a very small part of the vast, complex system of energy and material exchange called Life on Earth. To pretend otherwise—or worse, to act as if the reverse were true—is both shortsighted and ultimately suicidal." As the sounds of the gulls and children on the beach below drifted up with the wind, she paused and stared intently at me for a long moment. "There is another aspect to this, an ethical consideration for two very large constituencies that typically have little or no representation in your halls of congress, your town councils, your corporate boardrooms, and your family dinner tables, and whose lives are radically affected by the decisions you make. I'm speaking of salmon, bear, coral reef, and tortoise, of the billions of microbes that inhabit any cubic foot of topsoil, of all the nonhuman species that literally comprise the basis and context of your own life. I also refer to the children—not just yours and your neighbors', but the Russian and Chinese and Peruvian and Ugandan children, and of all their children yet unborn, the billions of human beings whose well-being depends very much on the choices you make in this pivotal time."

39

Living Traditions and the Original Green

Stephen Mouzon

Can traditional architecture be green? The question arises from what would appear to be a great weakness of modernism: the movement was born at the beginning of the Thermostat Age and is based on a love affair with all things mechanical. Modernist architecture has historically consumed more energy per square foot of building than any other architecture ever conceived throughout all of human history. Copious consumption actually lay at the foundations of the movement because it represented liberation wrought by the machine from natural limitations of the old orders. Staying warm in winter, holding up the roof, and getting to work were suddenly much easier, and the modernists intended to celebrate those facts. Le Corbusier famously said, "I shall live 30 miles from my office in one direction, under a pine tree—my secretary will live 30 miles away from it too, in the other direction, under another pine tree. We shall both have our own car. We shall use up tires, wear out road surfaces and gears, and consume oil and gasoline."

Today's "Techno Greens" are modernist architects who have risen up against this seemingly bleak background. Techno Greens base their work on the principles of "Gizmo Green," the proposition that sustainability may be achieved using nothing more than better materials and mechanical gizmos. The Techno Greens often produce modernist buildings that are actually efficient. And because it is so completely against the nature of modernist architecture to be green, whenever they succeed, there is an intriguing story to tell. Trade publications, of course, have happily complied, telling the story of Gizmo Green as if it were the only green alternative. After all, it sells lots of magazines.

But the story of sustainability is much bigger than Gizmo Green. If we insist on plainspoken definitions of words, then *sustainable* must mean "keeping things going for a very long time." Places can be sustainable if they are Nourishing, Accessible, Serviceable, and Secure. Once the *place* is sustainable, it is possible to talk about constructing sustainable *buildings*, which should be Lovable, Durable, Flexible, and Frugal. These are the eight foundations of sustainability.

If buildings last for a very long time, then their Frugality is more meaningful. Frugality occurs both as a result of the mechanical devices we use and also the passive design techniques that require no machines at all. Gizmo Green is a part of Frugality, but not the whole story. Clearly, because it is only a fraction of one of the eight foundations of sustainability, Gizmo Green is a very small part of true sustainability. The combination of sustainable buildings built in sustainable places constitutes the "Original Green." Before the Thermostat Age, buildings in which people spent more than a couple of hours per day had no choice but to be green. Otherwise, people would freeze to death in

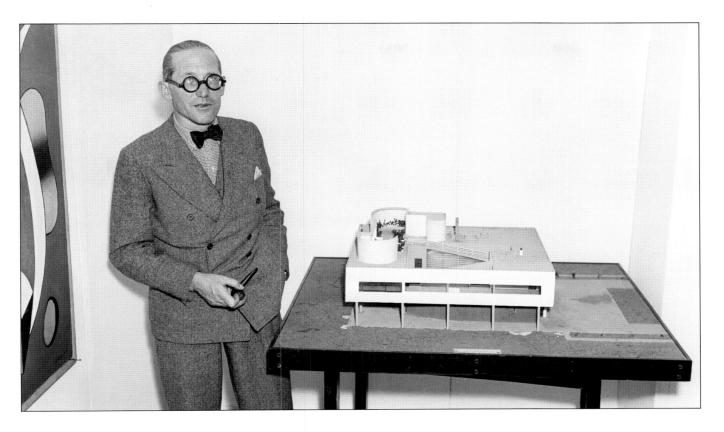

Left: *French architect Le Corbusier with an architectural model of his Villa Savoye, built in a suburb near Paris.*

Left: *Techno Greens often produce buildings that are actually efficient. But it's easy not to: this building is surrounded by surface parking lots, has no windows, it looks like an inefficient building despite the photovoltaic panels on the roof.*

winter, die of heat strokes in summer, or other dreadful things would happen to them. One could shiver for an hour or two in a cathedral and survive, but spending night after night there in the dead of winter could be a far different matter.

The Original Green was not about style at all. The vast majority of humanity's most sustainable places were likely built by people who cared little about style. Their proposition for how and why they built what they built

could be characterized simply as "this is how we build here." That is a far cry from building based on the prospects of getting published in the latest hot periodical. Original Green was ultimately empirical, and ultimately pragmatic: it was simply doing the things that made the most sense in a particular place.

Today, the Original Green places that best survived the destruction of all things not modern over the past century form the bulk of the Most-Loved Places on earth. The best of them draw millions of tourists from around the world. As a matter of fact, the entire world tourism industry is based almost exclusively on the Most-Loved Places. How did Original Green places come to be the world's Most-Loved Places? They did so through the mechanism of Living Traditions.

Living Traditions

A Living Tradition begins as a great idea by a single person. Normally, it's a great idea about solving a single place-making or building-making problem. The person builds the idea, and if successful, they build it again and again so that it becomes a personal pattern. If other people in the place it was first built see the personal pattern and it resonates with them, they copy it. Copied enough, it becomes a local pattern. Once a local pattern is established, it will be seen by others in the region around the place where it was first built. If it resonates enough with the citizens of the region, they say, "We love this. We want to adopt it into our family of built traditions." The tradition, thus adopted, may live on for centuries or occasionally even millennia after the person who created it has died. The length of the life of the tradition is directly proportional to how much it continues to be loved by the citizens. So Living Traditions, by definition, are those things that are most worthy of love. And they persist and spread in an organic fashion according to how vigorously they resonate with people.

Living Traditions replicate because they resonate, and they also have the ability to carry a lot of wisdom in their genetic code. Much of this wisdom exists just below the level of conscious thought. An eave may remain vigorous in a region because it is considered beautiful, long after most citizens have forgotten that it developed after a long period of trial and error to determine the best response to the sun angles, precipitation, and wind conditions of that region. But while it persists because it is beautiful, it is still delivering all of the wisdom that was embedded in the pattern while it was being developed.

Living Traditions are wonderfully efficient ways to pass down reams of wisdom to the next generation without requiring every member of a culture to have a graduate-level understanding of architecture. Living Traditions have performed this task worldwide for millennia. No alternative mechanism has ever been developed or tested that can operate on a culture at large and pass down massive amounts of wisdom without the receivers of that wisdom actually learning the particulars of that wisdom in great detail. Our system of higher education passes down a great deal of wisdom, but only to those students who are willing to dedicate years of their lives at great expense to learn a particular discipline.

Living Traditions pass down wisdom on the patterns of how we build. They can be grouped into three general categories: regional conditions, climate, and culture. The regional conditions include things like special weather events such as hurricanes or typhoons that are not part of the normal climate. They also include the locally available materials, the regional skill sets, the local topography, and the local geography. Climatic conditions include the annual range of temperature, precipitation, humidity, wind, or some combination of these. Cultural conditions include preferences for color, pattern, or other detail. Two of the three categories (regional conditions and culture) contribute directly to

the sustainability of the places that we build, while the third (cultural preferences) supports sustainability by making the patterns especially Lovable to the people that live there. Living Traditions of places and buildings do not randomly happen to pass down sustainable patterns from time to time. Rather, the fundamental reason that Living Traditions exist is to pass down wisdom on how to live for generations in a place with an economy of means. Put another way, Living Traditions are humanity's fundamental delivery mechanism for sustainability.

Above Top: *Longhouse in the Sarawak Cultural Center complex. There are more than 4,500 longhouses in Sarawak, Malaysia.*

Above Bottom: *Old stone and sod house at Arnol, Isle of Lewis. Climatic conditions and local materials lend themselves to this building approach.*

vigorous and vocal condemnation of tradition, such as Adolph Loos' proclamation, "Ornament is sin." Modernism, however, merely finished the job.

Death by Specialization

Prior to industrialization, most people played dual roles as specialists and as generalists. They would specialize in an activity that could earn them outside income, but they would build their own buildings, make their own clothes, raise their own food, and make many of the other artifacts of everyday life. A few extraordinarily intelligent or talented people could live entirely off of their specialty, but most could not afford to buy all the things they needed from the income derived from their specialty. But the great efficiency of industrialization changed all of that in at least two ways. By building things much more efficiently, they became cheaper. Moreover, the industrial worker could contribute to the production of many times more of particular goods or services working in the factory than by providing those same goods or services by hand at home.

At first, the industrial barons kept nearly all of the wealth, and the workers hardly fared better than they would have as subsistence farmers. But the rise of the labor movement changed the equation dramatically, so that it actually became possible for the general population to become specialists in one activity and trade the income derived from that activity for all of their daily needs of goods and services.

There were, however, at least two serious unintended consequences of complete specialization as it applies to the places we make and the buildings we build: If those places and those buildings are things we buy from specialists rather than places and buildings that we help to build ourselves, then we have no authority to tell the specialists of places and buildings that what they are providing is not good enough, because they are

Above: *Thatcher at work on roof. This is a highly skilled, specialist job.*

The Death of Tradition

Today, Living Traditions of places and buildings exist almost nowhere in the industrialized world. Modernism gets most of the blame (or credit, depending on your position) for destroying tradition because of its adherents'

presumed to know far more about places and buildings than we do. They make places and build buildings all the time, and we do not do it at all. How could we possibly have any authority in that situation?

The second unintended consequence is that specialists tend to know more and more about less, leading to the condition of knowing absolutely everything about just one thing. Ultimate specialization precludes a holistic approach.

It is the combination of these two unintended consequences of specialization that has conspired to destroy Living Traditions: if you have no authority to tell a specialist that what they are producing is not good enough, and if they are focusing on smaller and smaller aspects of what they are producing, then it is inescapable that those products, while they may be produced very efficiently, could not possibly address the complete range of human needs that were addressed when generalists previously made those products.

Death by Modernism

Modernism was in its ascendency just as specialization was completing its transformation of industrialized cultures worldwide after World War I. This is not coincidental, as modernism would not have been possible in a culture populated primarily with generalists. Modernism has never been loved by the majority of the world's population. If there is any doubt, look at what people choose for their own houses: by an overwhelming majority, people in most places will choose the styles of traditions that once lived, even if they are poorly executed, over any modernist style, even if its execution is excellent. So how could modernism complete the destruction of Living Traditions if it is so soundly rejected by the people?

Modernism originated as a movement of great optimism, fulfilling the promise of the Industrial Revolution to all. This rapturous euphoria over the promise of all things new sweeping away the old ossified orders was extremely seductive. In short order, almost all architects who had any aspirations of greatness converted to modernism. The list of notable traditional architects to make the switch is long. Even Frank Lloyd Wright, then in his sixties, completely remade himself beginning with Fallingwater.

Below: A view of Fallingwater, a house created by the famous architect Frank Lloyd Wright.

Architects took their role as specialists seriously on several counts. Decades of efforts to make architecture a licensed profession were paying off, and generalists (nonarchitects) were no longer able to design anything except their own houses. This single factor of architect registration effectively removed over half of all buildings from the reach of generalists, and of Living Traditions, under penalty of law. The registration movement was sold as a noble effort to protect the public health, safety, and welfare. This is not entirely inaccurate, because the industrial building materials created by other specialists really did need more attention to detail than the less-processed materials of traditional architecture. But the irony is that today, nearly a century later, when people choose a holiday destination because of its beauty, that destination is overwhelmingly likely to have been designed by people who were not licensed architects, but were generalists instead, just building their cities and towns.

There remains, however, an aspect of modernism that was perhaps more of a fatal blow to Living Traditions than any already discussed. Modernism might be seen as a large collection of the personal styles of heroic architects, united by little more than their desire to be nontraditional. The antitraditionalism, which has varied within modernism from vigorous to virulent, might be seen as the biggest culprit in the burial of Living

Traditions, but this is just superficial. The real reason that modernism completed the destruction of Living Traditions rests with the underlying principle that united this loose collection of architects into a coherent movement: modernism is built in part on the proposition that if you want to be significant, you must be unique. This sounds harmless at first. After all, would this tenet not encourage creativity? What could be wrong with encouraging architects to be more creative?

The problem with requiring uniqueness is that by disallowing patterns that already exist, each significant architect must invent his or her own style. Architecture, in effect, totally abandoned its centuries-long evolutionary model in favor of a series of little revolutions—so little, in fact, that the revolutions were confined to the work of a single architect. This requirement arguably continues to do more damage to the possibility of Living Traditions than all the rest because it doesn't just disallow the handing down of wisdom as an unintended consequence of another act. Rather, it flies directly in the face of the handing down of wisdom, declaring it to be without significance.

Sustainability and Living Traditions

Because the fundamental definition of sustainability is the ability to keep things going for a very long time, it should be clear that Living Traditions, which are able to span generations, centuries, and even millennia, are far superior delivery devices of sustainability than those that have shorter life spans. The opposite is clearly illustrated today, as almost the entire industrialized world is working furiously to figure out how to build and live sustainably before we face greater consequences than we have seen to date. It is clearly a difficult task, because while the great effort of the best minds in the world is being expended, we are nowhere near success yet. We have not yet even managed to live with the carbon footprint of our parents, much less with that of our eighteenth-century ancestors.

There are two fundamental roadblocks. The lack of the timeless shortcut of Living Traditions to pass implicit wisdom down embedded in beauty means that we must actively relearn the details of each detail of sustainability. This is an enormous effort. And then we must teach that wisdom to millions. Because the effort is so huge, there is not an encouraging likelihood of success before the onset of more onerous damage to our planet.

Foundations of Original Green
Sustainable Places

Original Green, fueled by Living Traditions, is humanity's natural mechanism for delivering true sustainability. The sustainability of buildings is meaningless unless the buildings are built in sustainable places. Sustainable Places, as previously noted, are Nourishing, Serviceable, Accessible, and Secure.

Nourishing Places

Nourishing Places grow a significant portion of their food within a few miles, and could grow more in a long emergency. The ingredients of an average meal in the U.S. travel over 1,300 miles to get to your table today, which means that very few places in the United States are Nourishing. As the industrialization of China and India continues, resulting in a billion new cars competing for gas over the next several years, the cost of food transportation will become much more significant.

Nourishing Places cannot be built in most places today owing to the shallow inflections in real estate value. Because we can drive for miles in a short period of time, we tend to value farmland the same as developable land in town a few miles away. This means that farmland is easily gobbled up for new development. In order to be able to look from a town to the fields where much of your food is

" Modernism is built in part on the proposition that if you want to be significant, you must be unique. "

47

raised, conditions must be developed that allow for sharp inflections in real estate value at the edge of town.

The most promising development leading to Nourishing Places is an effort over recent decades to make agriculture more compact. Large-scale agriculture is very labor efficient, allowing huge quantities of food to be raised using very few laborers, but it does not use land as efficiently. Bio-intensive methods, however, some of which have existed for centuries, allow all of the food needs of one person to be met on as little as one-tenth of an acre, and that efficiency is increasing. This capability will be essential once we figure out how to preserve that farmland near a town.

Below: Accessible Places are those where you have a choice of how to get around.

Accessible Places

Accessible Places are those where you have a choice of

how to get around. If you can choose to drive, walk, bike, or take the train, then you can do what makes the most sense. If you can only drive, then you have no choice, nor do any of the other people clogging the highway ahead of you. New urbanism has developed many tools over the past three decades to deliver transportation choice. And that choice must prefer self-propelled methods above those that are driven by engines, because transportation choice isn't just about using less fuel; it must also include the option of using no fuel at all. The benefits of walking and biking go beyond saving fuel, as they are the only modes of transportation that actually make you healthier. This is the one foundation of Sustainable Places that can realistically be positioned as having been solved.

Serviceable Places

Serviceable Places are those that provide the basic services of life within walking distance, so that driving is a choice, not a necessary fact of survival. Serviceable Places also accommodate the people who serve you, such as firefighters, police, and teachers, either somewhere in the neighborhood or in nearby neighborhoods so that their daily commute can be a walk or a bike ride if they choose, rather than the fifty-mile drive currently required in many increasingly unaffordable places across the country. The largest remaining challenge is figuring out how to provide affordable homes for the people who are servicing you. Where will our kids be able to afford a home when they get out of college? They

Above: The Boston City Hall and its adjoining plaza, Government Center.

New urbanism has for years advocated open networks of streets connecting all places; if a development has a gate, it's not considered to be new urbanism. But the time has come to have a rational conversation about ways of having a secure edge to neighborhoods within a city, and to hamlets, villages, and towns in the landscape. This secure edge must solve the problems that today's gated communities leave unsolved. But if we succeed in figuring out how to build Secure Places again, then we will create the added benefit of making places that stand out against the rolling same-ness of sprawl that renders much of the fabric of cities from Denver to Des Moines to Dallas to Durham indistinguishable one from another.

Foundations of Original Green

Sustainable Buildings

It is only when we have made our places sustainable that we can focus on ways of making sustainable buildings within them. A building might operate totally off the grid, creating all of its own energy onsite, but if it is located in a place where you must drive to meet all of your daily needs, then the total carbon footprint of living there may still be high.

Lovable Buildings

Any serious conversation about sustainable buildings must begin with the issue of Lovability. If a building cannot be loved, then it is likely to be demolished and carted off to the landfill in only a generation or two. All of the embodied energy of its materials is lost if they are not recycled. And all of the future energy savings are lost, too. Buildings continue to be demolished for no other reason than that they cannot be loved. Even an architectural landmark as celebrated as Boston City Hall is in danger of this fate because only an architect could love it.

Some in the green building community are now advocating that every building should have a plan for its

will live in this "Next-Generation Housing" and these "Next-Generation Neighborhoods."

Secure Places

Secure Places once built walls to assist in repelling armed attackers (see page 49). These walls also caused a sharp inflection in property values, because a home just inside the wall was clearly of much greater value than a home just outside. This helped preserve farmland outside the gates, which is a necessary element of Nourishing Places.

Today the problem is more complex because those most likely to do you physical harm or to make off with your belongings are not armed bands from a nearby town, but individuals or small teams of criminals that operate largely out of sight rather than at the gates. But it is no less important to figure this out, because how can a place be considered sustainable if those who live there are fearful?

eventual demolition and recycling. At first, this seems an honorable goal. But in reality, it is an admission of the inability to build in a Lovable fashion. Our ancestors once built for the ages, and the best of their buildings could last for a thousand years or more. Even the everyday buildings lining every street regularly lasted for centuries. A building that lasts for several centuries almost certainly outlasts the useful life of its component parts if they are demolished and rebuilt in different buildings, because building parts that remain in their original building clearly last longer than those that endure repeated demolitions and reassemblies.

Many ask today how it is possible to know what other people love, and some are even offended at the proposition that we might know what future generations might love. This suspicion is built upon the notion that

beauty is in the eye of the beholder, and is predicated upon the model of architecture as fashion.

But architecture can do so much better than that. Because that which is the most intensely "of our time" today is also the most quickly out-of-date tomorrow, if it is based solely on current architectural fashion. If we focus instead on what it means to be human rather than just what is popular in this moment, then it is clear that some things have resonated with humans throughout the ages.

So while it is not possible to guess what architectural fashions might be like in twenty or thirty human generations (or even next year, for that matter), it most certainly is possible to stack the deck in our favor by building things that incorporate patterns that reflect timeless aspects of our humanity. Doing so extends the efficiency of what we build today into the distant future.

Left: *This view shows that even the Paris Bourse de Commerce is adaptable— an icon of Flexibility.*

Durable Buildings

Our ancestors built for the ages. Their buildings were Durable enough to last for centuries, and because they were Lovable, they often did. Can we conceive of buildings that last for so long? Durability is essential to sustainability. Inexplicably, most so-called sustainable buildings today are still built of materials and in configurations that make it unlikely that they will last even a century.

Flexible Buildings

Within a Durable shell, a building must be extremely Flexible if it is to last for centuries. We cannot even conceive of how many uses a building might be put to in thirty or forty generations, which is how long buildings may last if they are both Lovable and Durable. So the interiors must be able to be recycled again and again for future uses that may not even exist today.

How is it possible to prepare for things that we cannot anticipate? Here is what we know, or at least believe that we know: the Durable shell of Flexible buildings should allow for attachment of interior improvements. Because our history over the past two centuries (with the exception of wireless Internet) has been one of increasing the number of pipes rather than decreasing them, Flexible buildings should have a strategy for channeling pipes through all of their rooms. Buildings can be used for more functions over time if they are closer to the street. Because our energy outlook over the next thousand years is most uncertain, buildings designed to be naturally Frugal will also be more Flexible. Buildings with low ceilings in hot climates, for example, may not be considered Flexible enough to save in the future, regardless of how Frugal they are today.

Frugal Buildings

Buildings can be considered Frugal in eight aspects: They can be Frugal with respect to the energy required to construct and operate the buildings, and the energy of the transportation associated with occupation of the buildings. They can be Frugal with respect to the materials used to construct the buildings, the recycling of the materials of construction and operation, and the stewardship of the water and air that surrounds the buildings. And finally, they are Frugal if the nature around them, and the wellness of the people who occupy them, is conserved.

Proponents of Gizmo Green are concerned with the energy required to construct buildings, and rightfully so. But Gizmo Green was born from a fascination with all things technical, and its practitioners prefer highly processed high-tech materials to traditional materials. The problem is that traditional materials generally contain much less embodied energy per pound than the high-tech ones. So while Gizmo Green makes some contributions to reducing the energy required to construct buildings by calling for materials extracted and formed regionally, Living Traditions do the same, and Living Traditions also prefer materials that have been processed less, embodying less energy.

The energy required to operate buildings is the measuring stick of Gizmo Green. Here, proponents of Gizmo Green have made large contributions. Unfortunately, those contributions focus heavily on the mechanical operation of the buildings, and because machines have a lifespan much less than a Durable building, they will eventually break down and need to be replaced. Our recent track record has been one of continually better machines, so it could be argued that eventual breakdown is actually a good thing, as it requires the machine to be replaced with a more efficient machine. But buildings created from Living Traditions that condition space first by passive means are more certain to work for the life of the building because passive means are not dependent upon any particular technology.

"Buildings created from Living Traditions that condition space first by passive means are more certain to work for the life of the building because passive means are not dependent upon any particular technology."

Transportation energy used during the construction phase increases the farther a product is manufactured from the building site; everyone agrees this should be reduced. But transportation energy used to operate the building after it is occupied is nowhere on the Gizmo Green radar screen.

Gizmo Green's proponents are rightly concerned about building with rapidly renewable materials or recycled materials. Living Traditions did this for millennia out of necessity, because a tradition that lived long enough to be passed down for generations obviously could not be built with materials that ran out in short order. The difference is that Living Traditions more easily use low-tech materials because they have no predisposition to the aesthetics of high technology.

Methods of recycling today have been almost completely defined by the proponents of Gizmo Green, and there is no downside to this. Credit should be given where it is due. Gizmo Green's proponents are also highly concerned with our stewardship of the water and air around us, and rightfully so. There are two downsides. Within buildings, when the mechanical systems fundamental to Gizmo Green design fail or are somehow compromised, then the entire building is likely to perform very poorly, if at all, until the parts arrive and the technician is able to install them. We have all likely

Below: *Windmill at Campo de Criptana, La Mancha, Spain. A Living Tradition, the windmill conserves resources.*

experienced a mechanically conditioned building rendered uninhabitable when its systems fail.

The next aspect of Frugality is our stewardship of that which remains natural around us. Gizmo Green proponents are again rightfully concerned with this issue and address it in a number of ways, such as the avoidance of light pollution and water pollution, recycling rather than consuming new construction materials, encouraging brownfield redevelopment, encouraging renewable energy, etc. New urbanism protects the environment by enticing people to live more compactly in order to leave more of nature untouched, and to pollute less by driving less. Living Traditions have always been based on making do with the materials and craft sets that are available regionally, and doing things in the least invasive way.

The final aspect of Frugality is that of conserving our own wellness: wellness of body, wellness of mind, and possibly even wellness of spirit. Gizmo Green addresses primarily chemical aspects of wellness of the body, such as proper ventilation to remove indoor pollutants and the use of building materials that are low in volatile organic compounds, which can vaporize and enter the atmosphere. New urbanism addresses physical wellness by encouraging walking, and also wellness of mind by providing for the creation of community. Living Traditions fulfill a broad range of wellness roles too comprehensive to list here that can best be encapsulated within the notion of engaging each person in a living process of achieving a sustainable way of life.

Frugality, as the last foundation of sustainable buildings, is considered the entirety of sustainability by many in the popular green movement. This is unfortunate. Not only is Frugality only one of eight foundations of sustainable places and sustainable buildings, but it is only partially addressed by Gizmo Green today, as illustrated above.

Deep Green Buildings

After a place achieves Original Green status, it can then go on to be "Deep Green" by generating power (especially electricity) onsite to fuel recent inventions such as computers and refrigerators that can be a part of a sustainable future. Because while we have recently found that some of the old solutions are better than some of the new, a Living Tradition is still all about finding the best ways to do something, whether old or new. Living Traditions are continually self-testing, using millions of minds. It seems, from this vantage point, that advances like computers and refrigeration are innovations that have actually made our lives better. And so, when such advances are found, a Living Tradition will find ways of accommodating and fostering them.

Fostering Life

The concept of Original Green is antithetical to architectural fashion because we have no way to guess what fashions might be like in a few years, let alone several centuries into the future. Living Traditions live because they resonate with regular people, and they replicate naturally, like other living things. These living ideas conserve resources because a Living Tradition does not rebuild just for novelty. But Living Traditions conserve more than resources. When a tradition lives across several generations, it develops a level of sophistication that is impossible with new inventions. Supporting a Living Tradition is an act of fostering life. It is far more efficient to plant an idea that can spread than to have to sell the idea again and again. The conclusion of the matter is this: that which can reproduce and live sustainably is green; that which is incapable of doing so is not green. This is the standard of life. Life is the process that creates all things green.

" Living Traditions conserve more than resources. When a tradition lives across several generations, it develops a level of sophistication that is impossible with new inventions. Supporting a Living Tradition is an act of fostering life. "

Left: *Houses and windmills at twilight in Oia, Santorini, Greece.*

Glossary

Accessible Places: Places that you can access through a variety of means, not just by car; self-propelled (pedestrian and bicycle) access is required; others are highly encouraged.

Durable Buildings: Buildings designed to have a Durable shell, even if the interiors are designed to be recycled repeatedly over time.

Flexible Buildings: Buildings designed to be adaptable to other uses in the future, including uses that do not currently exist.

Frugal Buildings: Buildings that use the energy of construction, materials of construction, energy of operation, materials of operation, and transportation associated with construction and operation in a frugal manner, and that are good stewards of the air and water around the buildings, the nature around the buildings, and our own wellness.

Gizmo Green: The sustainability ideas and methods espoused by the Techno Greens; the solutions of which are primarily limited to better equipment and better materials.

Living Tradition: A tradition that, similar to a living spoken language, is in regular use by all the citizens of the region in which it is found.

Lovable Buildings: Buildings designed to be loved by focusing on timeless principles humans have always been known to appreciate rather than the latest architectural fashions.

Modernism: A collection of architectural styles specific to single architects or small groups of architects united in their varying degrees of rejection of all things traditional.

Most-Loved Places: Those places around the world that have been loved the longest and are usually valued the highest; Most-Loved Places pass the Tourist Test.

New Urbanism: A set of principles for building places made up of neighborhoods that are compact, diverse, and walkable.

New Urbanist: A person who promotes and/or practices the principles of the new urbanism.

Next-Generation Housing: Homes that are affordable to recent college graduates.

Next-Generation Neighborhoods: Neighborhoods that include a proportion of Next-Generation Housing that is similar to the proportion of people in the area who earn entry-level wages.

Nourishing Places: Places where you can look out onto the fields or onto the waters from which a significant portion of your food comes.

Original Green: A concept defined by a holistic set of principles that creates sustainable places (which are Nourishing, Accessible, Serviceable, and Secure) in which sustainable buildings (which are Lovable, Durable, Flexible, and Frugal) may be built.

Secure Places: Places in which the residents are not regularly under undue fear for their lives, safety, or the safety of their belongings.

Serviceable Places: Places where you can walk to your daily necessities within or adjacent to your own neighborhood; also, where those serving you those services can afford to live.

Techno Greens: Architects who believe that sustainability may be achieved either completely or primarily through technical means.

Thermostat Age: The era that began with the invention of mechanical heating, which allowed people to condition their buildings with the touch of a button.

Tourist Test: Is a place good enough that people come from far away to visit it for the delight of being there, rather than to visit friends or to be entertained? If so, then it may be one of the Most-Loved Places.

Suggested Reading

A Pattern Language. Christopher Alexander, Oxford University Press, 1977. This book is considered by many to be "the Bible of new urbanism."

A Vision of Britain: A Personal View of Architecture. HRH The Prince of Wales, A. G. Carrick Ltd., 1989. A book written fairly early in HRH The Prince of Wales' career as a healer of places; it includes some of the fundamental ideas upon which his current principles of sustainable places are built.

Architecture: Choice or Fate. Léon Krier, Andreas Papadakis Publisher, 1998. This theoretical work encompasses both the urban scale and the architectural scale. Intriguing read.

Architecture Without Architects: A Short Introduction to Non-Pedigreed Architecture. Bernard Rudofsky, Hacker Art Books, 1969.

Charter of the New Urbanism. Congress for the New Urbanism, McGraw-Hill, 2000. A 194-page expansion on the original 27-point Charter of the New Urbanism, written by the founders.

New Urbanism: Comprehensive Report & Best Practices Guide. Robert Steuteville, Philip Langdon, and special contributors, New Urban Publications, 3d ed., 2003. This is the absolutely essential catalog of the current planning techniques of the new urbanism.

Suburban Nation. Andrés Duany, Elizabeth Plater-Zyberk and Jeff Speck, North Point Press, 2000. The essential description of how we got the place we call America and what we can do about it, by the founders of the new urbanism. Excellent read.

The New Urbanism, Toward an Architecture of Community. Peter Katz, McGraw-Hill, 1994. This is the early catalog of the emerging new urbanism, and covers the pioneering developments. Still a best-seller after more than a decade.

The Timeless Way of Building. Christopher Alexander, Oxford University Press, 1979. This is the absolutely essential precursor to *A Pattern Language*.

CHAPTER 4

Tradition and Innovation in Green Architecture and Urbanism

Prof. James Steele

Vernacular architecture around the world is nothing less than a key to future survival, holding countless valuable secrets that have been painstakingly accumulated over centuries in response to different global environmental conditions. The background to the expanding public knowledge about the connection between indigenous architecture and ecology is extensive, but in a broad and brief outline it begins in the late 1960s and early 1970s.

The first Earth Day on April 22, 1970, evidenced a consensus about ecology that arose out of the fractious and socially conscious 1960s and that seemed prescient when oil supplies were cut and prices drastically increased in 1973. Public anger prompted some conservation efforts, but little else. A report entitled *Limits to Growth*, published in 1972 by a G6 (later G8) consortium called the Club of Rome, focused on the fact that global industrial activity was increasing exponentially, and predicted drastic consequences if such growth were not altered. This report is now seen as naive, but it succeeded in popularizing the idea of "zero growth."

All of the environmental issues raised on that first Earth Day—resource degradation, population growth and agricultural limits leading to global famine, pollution of air and water, the disastrous potential climatic effect of the concentration of greenhouse and ozone-depleting gases in the atmosphere, and their corollaries—have now

been presented to the public in exhaustive detail. Incontrovertible evidence of the irreparable damage being inflicted on the planet mounts daily. The subtle but significant philosophical shift that has taken place since 1970 has been an emphasis on the concept of sustainability rather than ecology, which has important implications in this discussion about green architecture and urbanism.

The first use of the word *sustainability* in connection with the environment occurred in 1980, in a publication produced by the International Union for the Conservation of Nature (UCN) in Switzerland entitled *World Conservation Strategy*, which inextricably linked sustainability to development. This report was intended to defuse the pro-growth-anti-growth debate that had raged throughout the 1970s between those who argued that economic progress was necessary in order to finance environmental protection and those who were against such growth because its inevitable result was resource degradation and waste. However, *World Conservation Strategy* had a limited impact on governmental policy.

The Brandt Commission

The Brandt Commission, named after Willy Brandt, who was then also chair of the Social Democratic Party of the Federal Republic of Germany, was a more effective

initiative. In a speech delivered in Boston in January 1977, Robert S. McNamara, who was then the president of the World Bank, proposed the formation of a Commission on International Development, to be chaired by Brandt. He repeated this request during his address at the annual meeting of the International Monetary Fund and the World Bank in Washington later that same year. As a result, a private independent commission was formed and held its first meeting in Germany in December 1978. Its twenty-person membership reflected McNamara's intent for it not to be dominated by representatives from industrialized countries. In 1980, after ten meetings, the commission produced a report entitled *North-South: A Program for Survival*. The report contained recommendations for changes in the operational procedures and policies of the International Monetary Fund and the World Bank with regard to sustainability.

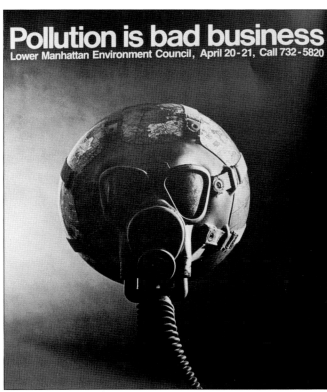

Above and Left: *Crowds on carless Fifth Avenue, as New York enjoys the first Earth Day.*

In retrospect, the Brandt Commission was little more than a thinly veiled promotional device to encourage developing world borrowers to seek more loans, continuing the destructive spiral of dependence. Its focus on the oil-producing countries and its somewhat abstract attitude toward the extremity of the adverse aspects that trade inequities were having throughout the developing world make it suspect. Yet it did initiate awareness of the need for global consensus and coordination on environmental policy through tactics such as "global negotiations" to be carried out at the United Nations. Through its emphasis on trade and finance in the developing world, the commission increased the focus on the need for rapprochement between economics and ecology that was to follow.

The Brundtland Commission

The gap between the growth and no-growth factions was finally bridged by the World Commission on Environment and Development, which was established by the United Nations as a strategic means of compromise between them. The proceedings of the commission, entitled *Our Common Future*, were published in 1987. The Brundtland Report, named after its chairperson, Norwegian Prime Minister Gro Harlem Brundtland, refined the concept of sustainability. The commission construed it as the principle that economic growth can and should be managed to ensure both the natural resources and the quality of life of future generations. Sustainable development was defined as "those paths of social, economic and political progress that meet the needs of the present without compromising the ability of future generations to meet their own needs."

The use of such a subjective word as *needs* left the concept open to critical interpretation, leading to speculation about whether it related to manufactured or natural assets. In spite of a vagueness on this central issue, the report held out the prospect of the perpetual satisfaction of human needs within a satisfactory natural framework, providing a compelling vision of the middle ground that could be attained.

By proposing that environmental health and economic growth are potentially compatible objectives, sustainable development offered a welcome relief from the paradigm of conflict that had characterized the debate on limits of growth during the 1970s. Sustainability moved to the forefront of the political debate about the feasibility of development.

Economic Roots

The concept of sustainability, then, is inextricably linked to development and, by extension, to economics. From the outset, the Brundtland Commission sought to arrive at a determination of the impact of development by holding community hearings in key industrialized countries to gauge public opinion. The U.N. commission was made up of political rather than environmental notables. They had a different agenda: to combine rather than separate issues about the environment and development, to show how this goal might be achieved globally, and to bring environmental policy into the political arena. The efficacy of extending production by using more efficient technology and conservation, the need to reduce the growth of worldwide population, and the definition of a mechanism that would allow the redistribution of resources from profligate countries (predominantly in the northern hemisphere) to the poor (predominantly in the south), were also adopted as articles of faith.

These positions recognized the fact that, since the beginning of the twentieth century, the industrially rich countries have thrived at the expense of the poorer ones and have caused most of the environmental damage now evident. This revealed the hypocrisy of the expectation that the developing nations, which are now industrializing,

" Since the beginning of the twentieth century, the industrially rich countries have thrived at the expense of the poorer ones and have caused most of the environmental damage now evident. "

Baghdad, for example, were traditionally built of stone to provide the thermal mass necessary to hold the sun's heat at bay during days in which the outside temperature could reach 125 degrees Fahrenheit. Their design included a basement with thick masonry walls that was intended to capture the cooler, heavier night air, which fell into it like water into a cistern, through a vent in the floor of the central courtyard. Secondary vents opening into shafts serving the rooms above were opened as the house heated up during the day, and the cold air in the basement, which rose as it became warmer, kept the interior temperature at about 68 degrees Fahrenheit on the hottest days.

This is only one of the ingenious examples of convective cooling in a historical context, yet it is one that is still to be replicated in contemporary terms. The fact that it was uniformly applied to all houses in the city, not to just one, is an indication of the scale of the collective—as opposed to specialized or professional—knowledge involved.

Medieval Cairo: A Self-Regulating City

A fascinating incidence of this collective consciousness also occurs in the medieval quarter of Cairo. The old center of Cairo is officially known as Gamaliyya, and is defined on the north by the Bab al Futuh and Bab al Nasr gates, on the south by the Ibn Tulun Mosque, on the east by the escarpment of the Moqattem Hills, the cemetery, and Saleh Salem Highway, and on the west by Port Said Street. The heart of the district is Al-Qahira

Above: *Sultan Hassan mosque with towering minarets and bulbous domes, as seen from Old Cairo's Citadel.*

Houses in Al-Fustat had a central courtyard with a fountain and two T-shaped *iwans*—vaulted halls open on one end—with portico fronts facing into it. This *iwan*-portico-courtyard relationship is the same as that seen in Ukhaidir Palace built in Iraq in the eighth century, where the north- and south-facing *iwans* were alternatively used to take best advantage of the breeze during the summer and the summer warmth in the winter. The similarity between the two arrangements indicates that this typology was introduced into Egypt from Iraq during the Tulunid dynasty.

The same configuration turns up again in Fatamid Cairo in revised form, transferred from exterior to interior space in response to socioeconomic forces and a growing desire for greater privacy from increasing urban pressure. This transformation came about through a wish for protection from direct exposure to the elements and concern about the noise from the rabble beyond the courtyard wall.

In its introverted version, the central courtyard became a recessed central square area called a *durqa'a*, which was covered by a high tower and flanked by two low-roofed *iwans* on its north and south sides. The entire ensemble is called a *qa'a*. A wind catch, or *malkaf*, was then added to its design. The degree of environmental control achieved by this single modification is dramatic, as tests run in 1973 by an investigative team from the Institute of Third World Studies at the Architectural Association in London demonstrated. Their study, carried out at a house called Mohibb al-Din, determined that the builders of the wind catch first oriented it toward the prevailing northerly breezes, controlling the amount of air channeled into it by opening the throat several degrees. The air that was thus directed into the central part of the *qa'a* was cooled even further by introducing a fountain into its floor.

As the air became warmer it began to rise into the high tower above the recessed central part of the space,

Above Top: *At Mohibb al-Din, the central courtyard became a recessed central square area called a* durqa'a.

Above Bottom: *Reception hall of Mohibb al-Din.*

Al-Fatima, or "Fatamid Cairo," the royal enclave established in A.D. 969 by Jawhar the Sicilian and used as an exclusive princely city from its completion in 974 until 1169. It was the last of five settlements stretching north along the Nile from the original military encampment of Al-Fustat.

winds as well as to thwart Turkish invaders, who brutally suppressed any hint of resistance by breaking into houses unexpectedly and punishing those suspected of involvement. The similarity of the exterior appearance of these houses, along with their anonymity, was at least some defense against this constant threat.

The anonymous white faces of the houses on this island, which are typically two stories high, have the functional advantage of reflecting sunlight and the internal heat it can cause, while the thick masonry walls help keep the inside cool as well. The white surfaces are the perfect foil for the way the light changes during the day, from the pinkish blue of early morning through the intense metallic glare at noon on a summer day, when the color of the sea seems to change from blue to liquid mercury. These color changes continue on through to dusk, when the intense heat turns the sky deep purple and the water matches Homer's description of a "wine dark sea."

Below: *The anonymous white faces of the houses on Mykonos, which are typically two stories high, have the functional advantage of reflecting sunlight.*

Global Champions

Advocates of the virtue of the traditional wisdom that is inherent in the built environment in Cairo and Mykonos were once considered to be pariahs by mainstream modernists. Even great talents like Alvar Aalto and Rudolph Schindler were considered suspect, because they embraced nature and favored telluric materials such as brick, wood, and stone rather than the inert and toxic industrialized palette of concrete steel and glass. The exclusion of the advocates of tradition was even more aggressive and far-reaching in the developing world, where progress was, and still is, viewed as the most essential ingredient in the process of development.

Now it seems that each nation in the world has at least one high-profile prophet who is promoting the value of tradition. In some places, including the United States, there are entire movements, such as the new urbanism, that are doing so. America has had its inspiring

Below: *Hassan Fathy created New Gourna in the late 1940s. This is the exterior of the adobe mosque in June 1955.*

individual champions as well, as among them the late Sam Mockbee, who founded the legendary Rural Studio in Alabama. The new urbanists have adopted a more far-reaching, systemic approach, attacking the collective built remnant of modernist principles at its root cause, proposing and supporting new legislation that overturns the exclusionary zoning of the past, which was based on the social primacy of industry.

But the most significant evolution in the attitude toward the value of the lessons inherent in worldwide vernacular architecture has occurred in Central and Western Asia. The sea change throughout this region has been driven as much by pride in a growing sense of identity as by concern about a loss of heritage, of going too far and too fast down the seductive, oil-slicked road of development after the embargo years of the 1970s. Huge revenues, far greater than those of the 1980s, admittedly continue to feed a penchant for spectacle, which has even spread beyond its most ostentatious epicenter in Dubai into the sacred confines of Makkah itself. But this trend has been offset by an equal and opposite initiative that is promoting the enduring values of tradition.

The most obvious examples of this direction are the disciples of Egyptian architect Hassan Fathy, who died in 1988 but left a powerful living legacy. Because of his long career, Fathy has had a direct influence on several generations of followers, not all of whom worked with him directly. Abdel Wahed El-Wakil, the most prominent member of the group, now has practices in the United Kingdom and most recently designed the Institute of Islamic Studies at Oxford. He achieved international recognition with an Aga Khan Award–winning house for the Halawa family in Agamy, Egypt. It was built in collaboration with Aladin Mustaffa, the Nubian mason who helped Fathy discover his essential principles. El-Wakil then focused on the Kingdom of Saudi Arabia, designing several mosques and houses there, most

notably the Al-Sulaiman Palace in Jeddah—a contemporary translation of the Jiddah Tower House.

Jordanian architect Rasem Badran has also been a prolific advocate of Fathy's ideas, translated to urban scale. He has demonstrated the efficacy of vernacular strategies in city form in his largest project to date: Qasr al-Hukm, in Riyadh. Qasr al-Hukm includes both a mosque and a palace, the interface of the sacred and the secular, as well as a more general commercial component.

The mosque and Palace of Justice of the Qasr al-Hukm complex are an attempt to awaken the values and memories of an important historical place with rich cultural, economic, social, and political legacies. Sensing its sacred history, Badran's initial reaction to the Qasr al-Hukm site was one of permanence. His goal was to retain its sacredness and reinforce its historical connection with the personification of secular authority, which has been an essential part of the cultural memory of the place. He also wanted to reestablish the strong relationship between the mosque and all other relevant activities of everyday life. The balance, in this case, between tradition and contemporaneity, is achieved by offsetting the sacred-secular equation, tempering the monumental aspect of the mosque and making the Palace of Justice seem less imposing. Harmony and equilibrium are skillfully and deliberately maintained. The mosque has a more approachable character. His instinct to strive for modesty rather than monumentality is in harmony with popular sentiment in the region and is a faithful representation of contemporary values.

In this era when the goal still seems to be one of scientific certainty and of using technology to solve a mounting litany of environmental problems, one of the most valuable lessons provided by the architecture and urbanism of the past is that certainty does not exist and that intuition is one of the most valuable of all human attributes.

"Now it seems that each nation in the world has at least one high-profile prophet who is promoting the value of tradition. In some places, including the United States, there are entire movements, such as the new urbanism, that are doing so."

The Four Greens

Andrés Duany

> "*Yes, the blame for climate change can be placed squarely on the design of the middle-class habitat, originally in North America, then the rest of the English-speaking world, and now disastrously exported to Eastern Europe, the Middle East, Latin America, and Asia.*"

It is always hard to believe that a very complex problem may have a root cause; and it is still more difficult if that cause is banal. Yet so it is with climate change. This blight that will consume the thought and the wealth of the twenty-first century has a single source: the lifestyle of the American middle class.

It is the way the middle class inhabits its buildings and settles the land, moves about, and entertains itself that is causing the damage. It is the pattern of suburban sprawl—associated with a dismal lifestyle of car dependence and its mitigation through consumption—that gobbles up natural resources and pollutes the earth. Yes, the blame for climate change can be placed squarely on the design of the middle-class habitat, originally in North America, then the rest of the English-speaking world, and now disastrously exported to Eastern Europe, the Middle East, Latin America, and Asia.

Why blame just the middle class? Do the truly wealthy not live the same? Perhaps so, but for all their visibility, they are too few to matter. And what of the poor? Are they not a problem? Well, the poor everywhere lead small lives—if unwillingly. They may not like it, but the poor usually dwell at high densities; they walk, bicycle, and use transit; they often grow their own food; they consume very little and they waste virtually nothing. Per capita their ecological footprint is a small fraction of that of the middle class.

Focusing on the middle-class habitat and its concomitant lifestyle is a necessary step in what will surely be the long march of environmentalism through the twenty-first century. Because climate change is a zero-sum game, the challenge is to convince *most* of those individuals to change their ways. One person's decision to live in a flat in downtown Indianapolis is neutralized by another's decision to purchase a suburban house in Inverness. This is different from the old campaigns for air quality or water quality—those could be effective within an airshed or watershed. This time it is the atmosphere *as a whole* that will affect temperature *globally* and cause *all* of the world's seas to rise concurrently. This crisis requires everyone to do their duty—and everyone, even within the narrow norms of the middle class, is not the same. Convincing the middle class to change its ways will be an exceedingly difficult proposition, as the middle class has something the poor do not: access to choice.

To give a relevant example: once a middle-class household qualifies for a mortgage loan, there are many dwellings available. A good number of them are suburban houses at some distance from shopping and workplaces, and there is always an automobile available to mitigate this distance. Furthermore, on a daily basis the middle class habitually drives right past nearby shops to others that are preferable. Schools, jobs, and entertainment are also chosen according to preference and not proximity. Even where excellent transit and withering gasoline prices are in place, an inordinate number of the middle class will put up with traffic to drive to whatever destination they like. With the exception of a few cities suffering from severe housing shortages, this middle class does not accept being told how and where to live, shop, and work, or how to get

around. Culpability tends to demoralize and even anger them, thus posing the difficulty that democratic leaders everywhere have in establishing limits. No democracy—not even Norway's, with its prominent green polemic and its North Sea oil-driven subsidies—is able to impose lifestyle changes that would be unpopular.

While a planned economy could achieve effective change, that kind of thing was attempted in postwar

Below: *The pattern of suburban sprawl: an aerial view of a housing development in Alameda County, California.*

Right and Opposite: *The poor usually dwell at high densities: shanty towns in Brazil (*Right*) and Mumbai (*Opposite*).*

Britain and no one who is sane would try it again—so environmentalists should not depend on it. Nor can we suppose that nature's gradually increasing wrath and the gradually dwindling petroleum reserves will compel most people to prevent the tipping point in time. Two decades of expertly managed fear-mongering, including first-rate visual aids, have convinced all too few, and so the metrics of climate change continue moving the wrong way. It should by now be evident that the green agenda must be more nuanced if it is to penetrate the consciousness of millions of self-interested individuals.

Fortunately, there is a place to turn for lessons. Indeed, convincing the diverse middle class to act in certain ways is the reason the vast and sophisticated marketing industry came into being. The first step of marketing is to identify market segments that reflect the diversity of the consumer. To connect effectively, the message—even the sacred environmental message—cannot be monolithic. It must be parsed to meet specific market segments, just as with any other idea or product (note the metamorphic "messages" of the recent U.S. presidential campaigns). The challenge is no longer with the substance of the environmental warning, which has been credibly nailed down by science. The challenge is with its packaging—some of which, believe it or not, should slyly promise self-esteem, style, profit, comfort, and even optimism. To paraphrase both George Bernard Shaw and Saul Alinsky: If the revolution is not appealing, no one will show up for the second meeting.

Environmentalists, justified in their higher morality and warranted in their impatience, can be rather hostile to this notion. But their preferred marketing of doom and gloom has proven effective primarily in eliciting lip service. Granted, it is a difficult situation, as the middle class worldwide seems to have learned from Americans to discount any message—indeed any reality—that interferes with their right to happiness, which, as James

Howard Kunstler puts it, is their continued participation in the "cheap oil fiesta."

To summarize: For environmental marketing, it is no longer a matter of refining the scary statistical evidence or providing more maps of the coming flood. It is a matter of better understanding the *consumers* of environmentalism. More than tinkering with the science, we must start tinkering with the message. As Christopher Alexander notes, "We all know what the appliance is . . . what we must do is design the plugs that will connect it to the existing power grids."

Fortunately, after decades of work, we now know what the "appliance" is. It was concurrently rediscovered, revived, conceptualized, applied, and promoted by Léon Krier in Continental Europe, by the Prince's Foundation and the Commission for Architecture and the Built Environment in the United Kingdom, and by the new urbanism and smart growth movements in the United States, Canada, and Australia. It consists of a type of human settlement that is compact, connected, complex, convivial, and as complete as possible. It thereby consumes less land and less energy, requires less transportation, and tends to fulfill leisure with sociability rather than consumption. It may have different names: the Urban Village in the U.K., the TND (traditional neighborhood development) and TOD (transit-oriented development) in the U.S., or the Quartier in the E.U., but it is the same thing: the fundamental human habitat—pervasive, cross-cultural, timeless—identifiable from the ruins of Pompeii to the *hutongs* of Peking.

The Urban Village is absent only where it has been overwhelmed by the specialized modernist analysis that knows only statistics and does not factor in externalities. This absence, of course, is also known as suburban sprawl, where the English-speaking middle classes and their worldwide imitators drive all the cars, throw too much away, and consume land and resources

" The challenge is no longer with the substance of the environmental warning, which has been credibly nailed down by science. The challenge is with its packaging— some of which, believe it or not, should slyly promise self-esteem, style, profit, comfort, and even optimism. "

Left: *Green Guru Al Gore speaks at a press conference before the Climate Project in Mexico City, September 29, 2009.*

disproportionately. They themselves are causing the climate change that will undermine their lifestyle, yet they do not consider themselves responsible, and certainly not evil. While many of them are simply oblivious, there are four groups who are already paying attention and may be addressed immediately. They are provisionally tagged *Ethicists*, *Trendsetters*, *Opportunists*, and *Survivalists*.

Ethicists

These are the heirs to the original environmentalists of the 1960s—the guardian class that has anointed itself as the protector of Mother Nature. Ethical to the core, they sometimes undermine their message by displaying the certainty of a higher morality. They do not understand how unpleasant it is to most people to be told that they

Left: *The emblem of the Ethicists: a polar bear mother and cubs.*

are malefactors. Their problem is that they have internalized the ethos that humanity is outside nature: that humans threaten the environment by their presence, that sin is measured by ecological footprint. These "green gurus" are the evangelists and activists who have learned to tap into the prestige of scientific metrics and have evolved into regulators. Because the subliminal message that humans are the problem is unpopular, they fall back on the top-down techniques of legal proscription, monitoring, and fines.

Their message is inadvertently Luddite, knowingly or unknowingly advocating for the impoverishment of a more austere time. A return to smaller dwellings, slower cars, no clothes dryers, unavailable off-season produce, and a smaller population are actually ideals to be desired. To their enormous credit, authentic Ethicists will voluntarily suffer these inconveniences of a more ecological lifestyle. Their personal example, when they practice what they preach, is very compelling. At best, they are our collective conscience, and they have provided the indispensable wake-up call. Nevertheless, given that they have been active for so long, and that the environmental situation is still dire, it is evident that the steady call for penance has not been an effective marketing tool. This may change with Al Gore, who is currently, brilliantly, their leader—if not their role model.

Above: *Cool Greens Bill Clinton (left) and actor Brad Pitt (right) pose before a groundbreaking ceremony for Pitt's "Make It Right" house construction project in the Lower Ninth Ward of New Orleans.*

Right: *The emblem of the Trendsetters: a Tesla electric sports car.*

Trendsetters

These are modern consumers who will make the environmental choice as long as it does not involve sacrifice. They may be only superficially environmental, but when these "cool greens" pick the next thing, it is likely to enter the mainstream quickly (local food is the current darling). They are viral marketers: when they decide canvas bags are fashionable, the stores will carry them (and they had better be well designed). They will drive economical cars and live in energy-efficient houses as long as they look really good. This is typified by the handsome second-generation Prius (no one bought the hideous first model) and the stylish *Dwell* magazine houses. They will eat organically if it tastes good, and they will recycle if it is convenient (while telling their friends all about it).

Trendsetters are not persuaded by the dour and demanding prescriptions of the Ethicists, falling instead for the optimism of the token efforts that are sometimes called "greenwash." This segment is nonetheless important because networks of peer groups will surely provide the critical mass for the tipping point. And they are now the target audience of the new green trend in the advertising industry, providing a tremendous multiplier effect to the cause. Someday, as with smoking, it will surely become uncool to waste and pollute. The environmental cause is well served by stars like Brad Pitt and his cool "Make It Right" houses.

Opportunists

These are economic pragmatists who thrive on environmental opportunities. Opportunists fall into the categories of providers and consumers: those profit-seeking entrepreneurs who incubate green businesses, and those who seek the savings of, say, reduced gas mileage, home-grown produce, or solar energy. Like the Trendsetters, their message is optimistic and infectious, trusting that progress—even breakthroughs—will pull us through the crisis. They are the "gadget greens," seeking technological fixes rather than cultural changes or moral choices. They are eager to tap the free market but not averse to accepting government subsidies and even a playing field tipped through regulation. They have a symbiotic relationship with the Trendsetters: The fabulous Tesla electric sports car, for example, is built by Opportunists and marketed to Trendsetters, and they are as quick to promote its impressive acceleration as they are

Left: *The emblem of the Opportunists: wind turbines near Cowley as a storm approaches from northwestern Alberta, Canada.*

Below: *Senator Robert Menendez (left) of New Jersey listens to Gadget Green T. Boone Pickens (right) during a news conference to introduce the New Alternative Transportation to Give Americans Solutions (NAT GAS) Act, which supports vehicles that run on natural gas. Washington, D.C., July 8, 2009.*

its great fuel mileage. This is not a trivial achievement, as it supports the prestige of electric cars as a whole.

Unlike the younger Trendsetters, Opportunists can be along in years, as required to capitalize large businesses like wind, solar, and tidal-energy generation (see page 81). At worst, they may detour us by stampeding to glamorous panaceas (as they did with corn ethanol), but they will attract the investment, enthusiasm, and creativity necessary to tackle the big technical problems. They may well succeed in the revival of genetic engineering and the restoration of the atomic power industry against the Luddite opposition of the Ethicists. The archetypal Opportunist is T. Boone Pickens (see page 81), but only because Sir Richard Branson is too cool to be a techno-nerd.

Survivalists

This group believes themselves to be the realists, that they are among the few who are cognizant of the inevitability of the coming bleakness. These "grim greens" have concluded that it is too late to halt or reverse climate change. In this they are supported inadvertently by the ever-scarier propaganda statistics put forth by the Ethicists. The Survivalists should be compatible in spirit with them, but they are resolutely local, having given up on the global situation. They expect climate change to lead to energy shortages, food scarcity, and social instability, but they are more likely to depend on community than were their bunkered predecessors of the Cold War era. Indeed, precisely because a global solution is intractable, they believe that the only effective response is to circle the wagons at the scale of community (the village, the compound, the family).

Survivalists will radically change their lifestyles—not like the Ethicists, for the sake of salvaging a benevolent and deserving nature (as symbolized by the polar bear cub), but to survive with their own offspring

Right: *Grim Green James Howard Kunstler.*

Below: *The Survivalists' emblem: Amish rebuild a barn destroyed by arson.*

Opposite and Left:
The Greenwich Millennium Village, London—a modern housing estate on an urban village model that transformed a former gas works—was designed by Ralph Erskine. The main sales pitches were: sustainable construction techniques; use of previously developed land in order to promote regeneration and minimize the amount of new land being taken for development; and drastic reductions in construction costs, energy/water consumption, and waste.

Bodies and Buildings:

Microcosm and Macrocosm in Traditional Architecture and Urbanism

Prof. David Mayernik

"*As the most perfect architecture, the human body offered a wealth of information about how to build well, and in concert with nature.*"

Figure 1: *Opposite: The human form and timber construction; after Leonardo da Vinci and the Manuale del Recupero del Comune di Roma. If we juxtapose Leonardo's drawings of the human shoulder with a diagram of the structure of a traditional timber roof, we see analogous forces of compression and tension, or pushing and pulling, animating each.*

Western culture once espoused a sympathetic relationship between human beings and the natural world (the "Four Elements") that many today associate with Eastern philosophy. Partly based on an instinctive anthropomorphism present in the cultures of Greece and Rome, and partly on a Judaic creation narrative coupled with a Christian conception of God-made Man, medieval and Renaissance Europe built environments that still serve as models for building well today because they strike us as sustainable, humanizing, and ennobling. As the most perfect architecture, the human body offered a wealth of information about how to build well, and in concert with nature. This sympathetic attitude continued to inform the language of urbanism and architecture well into the Enlightenment and beyond, until supplanted by the mechanistic metaphors of early modernism.

The specific and implied relationships between the human body and traditional building reveal the culture behind the buildings and cities we continue to use as models. Analogies between traditional buildings and the human body fostered environments that were healthy and sustainable for both buildings and people—both the formal analogies (for example, the anatomy of the shoulder and roof trusses, the circulation system and medieval street patterns) and the dynamics of use (circulation, walkable cities and buildings, ventilation and breathing), along with the poetics of microcosm and macrocosm (man as a small world, buildings as bodies). These principles are being put into practice again in modern building.

Such is the case in P. A. Barca's *Avertimenti e Regole* (1620), which recommended the use of square, pentagonal, or hexagonal fortifications since these figures were symbols of the relation between the human body and the cosmos. God, the divine architect, had created the heavens and the earth "with weight, number and measurement," conforming everything to the circle, the most perfect figure. Man, on the other hand, "is a small world. . . . His flesh is the earth, his bones are mountains, his veins are rivers, and his stomach is the sea." [1]

Seeing the world as a body, and the body as a world, fostered a sympathetic building culture for millennia that saw the creation of human environments that were harmonized with the wider world, and indeed were understood to be connected to the structure of all of creation. The tendency to anthropomorphize nature was directly tied to the anthropomorphism of buildings, as human beings built upon principles derived from their intuitive understanding of anatomy. Although this world view prevailed even in centuries when there was not much scientific knowledge of the workings of the body, it flourished consciously and more instructively with the Renaissance's focus on man as the measure of all things.

In Leonardo da Vinci's anatomical drawings we find a progressively deeper discovery of the structure underlying not only the human form, but human movement. Joints, muscles and tendons, and flesh *move* man the marvelous machine, and Leonardo the artist is specifically interested in representing the body (human, but also animal) in motion. If we juxtapose Leonardo's drawings of the human shoulder—focusing in this case on muscle and bone—with a diagram of the structure of a traditional timber roof, we see analogous forces of compression and tension, or pushing and pulling, animating each (Figure 1). This relationship may very well have been causal: in understanding how to make buildings stand up, early builders no doubt referred to their own lived experience of structure—the body—and its capacity to bear weight, create or resist forces, and fail under stress. There is an element of empathy in the tensile aspects of traditional timbering, and there is also a return on that investment in a building's capacity to help us understand human forces in action. This is how Homer described a wrestling match between Ajax and Odysseus:

> Both champions, belted tight, stepped into the ring
> and grappling each other with big burly arms,
> locked like rafters a master builder bolts together,
> slanting into a pitched roof to fight the ripping winds.[2]

If arms and shoulders could serve as analogies to timber framing, legs and feet furnished models of stability at the bases of buildings (Figure 2a). "Footings" under foundations and pedestals (etymologically derived from the Latin *pes*, or foot), and also the generally pyramidal nature of masonry construction (heavier and wider at the base), could be understood by an analogy with the body's greater stability, with feet firmly planted on the ground and legs spread slightly. Not only that, but the general sense of deformation when that stable body is loaded with extra weight translates into our empathetic understanding of buildings under load, expressed in the swelling of column shafts (*entasis*), the spreading of base

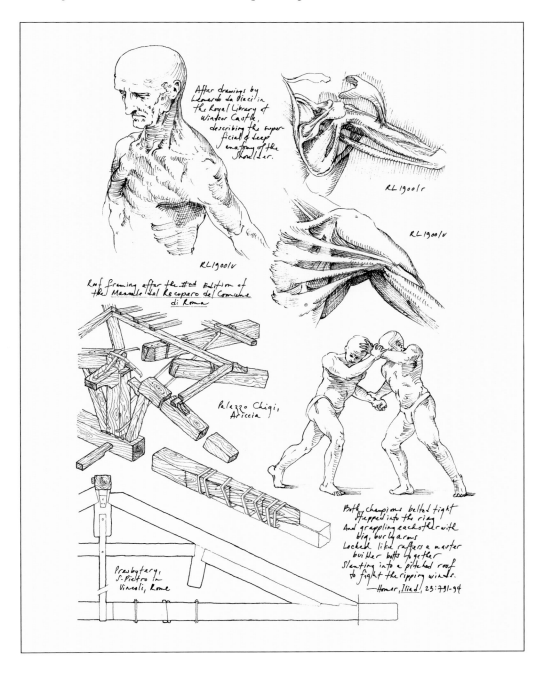

87

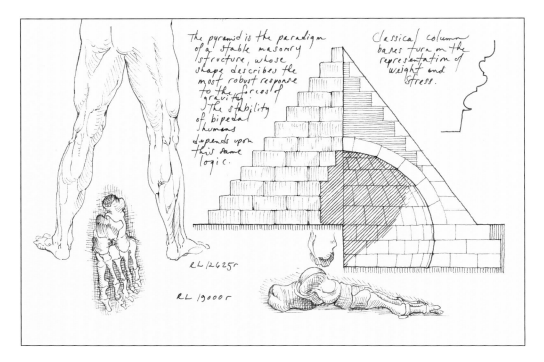

The pyramid is the paradigm of a stable masonry structure, whose shape describes the most robust response to the forces of gravity. The stability of bipedal humans depends upon this same logic.

Classical column bases turn on the representation of weight and stress.

RL /2625r

RL /9000r

Figure 2a: *Stability in the body and pyramids. If arms and shoulders could serve as analogies to timber framing, legs and feet furnished models of stability at the bases of buildings.*

moldings, or stepped water-table profiles. Again, this relationship worked two ways: the body helped builders understand how their construction would perform and deform under loads, while a sensitively designed building embodying these principles enabled the viewer or user to comfortably sense and even comprehend the building's stability, fostering an intuitive sense of well-being in an evidently stable environment.

Leon Battista Alberti employed the body analogy to explain masonry arches and vaults. Stressing the way that vaulting systems involving disparate layers and materials need to be integrated, he resorted to anatomy, and the layering of the body's bones, muscles, and skin:

> The same method of construction should be followed for the vaults as is used for the walls. In fact, the bones within the wall continue unbroken right up to the top of the vault; they are constructed in the same way and are set a correspondingly similar distance apart. The ligaments stretch from bone to bone, and the

section between is filled with paneling. . . . For the bones the ancients would almost always use baked bricks. . . . In short, with every type of vault, we should imitate Nature throughout, that is, bind together the bones and interweave the flesh with nerves running along every possible section: in length, breadth, and depth, and also obliquely across. When laying the stones to the vault, we should, in my opinion, copy the ingenuity of Nature.[3]

Figuratively, facades were naturally understood as faces, with the door as the mouth and windows as eyes. At once anthropomorphizing the building and providing an image of the inhabitant, these analogies could occasionally be made strangely explicit, as at the house of the artist Federico Zuccaro in Rome (now the Biblioteca Hertziana), where a literal mouth and eyes are described by the molded surrounds. Renaissance writers like Pietro Aretino maintained that one could judge a person's character equally well by their face and their house:

> But for anyone who wants to see how clean [*netto*] and bright [*candido*] is his spirit, let him look at his face [*fronte*] and his house; let him look at them, I say, and he will see what calm and what beauty one can contemplate in a house and in a face.[4]

The integration that the body's systems represented was a scalable analogy, applicable from construction of buildings to the layout of cities. In Leonardo's drawings of the body's circulation system we can see similarities to the street networks of ancient and medieval hill towns (Figure 2b). The ways in which the body distributes blood, with branching systems that accommodate supply and return, find parallels in the major and minor streets, working relatively with and against the contours of their sites, of towns like Todi, Voltera, or San Gimignano. Alberti specifically recommended winding streets only for smaller towns as a means to frustrate attackers. While the formally "organic" character of medieval towns would seem to suggest more direct comparisons with the body's systems, classical Renaissance planning on orthogonal or radial geometries were also, perhaps strangely to us, meant to be understood as mimetic of natural order (in this case of the underlying geometry of the cosmos, which gave proportion to both man and the heavens). Moreover, they were meant to more rationally distribute people in towns that were increasingly less concerned with defense, and therefore functioned like the body's arterial systems. Especially in the eighteenth century, discussions of urban planning in major cities like Paris referred to wide and rationally designed street networks as facilitating healthy circulation of bodies and air, tying the health of the city to the health of its citizenry. That analogy, wedded to his experience of garden design, was sustained by L'Enfant in his plan for Washington:

> By being out in the open air, a citizen, Jefferson said, breathes free: Jefferson applied this metaphor to the countryside, which he loved; L'Enfant applied it to the city. The medical origins of the metaphor suggested that, thanks to circulating blood, the individual members of the body equally enjoyed life, the most minor tissue as endowed with sanguine life force as the heart or brain.[5]

Vitruvius had insisted on the body as the model for the ideal temple, and by this he meant to express at least two fundamental ideas: that the frontal body was symmetrical about its vertical axis, and that it had a precisely ordered relationship between its parts and the whole. This mapping of the body onto the plans of temples would be

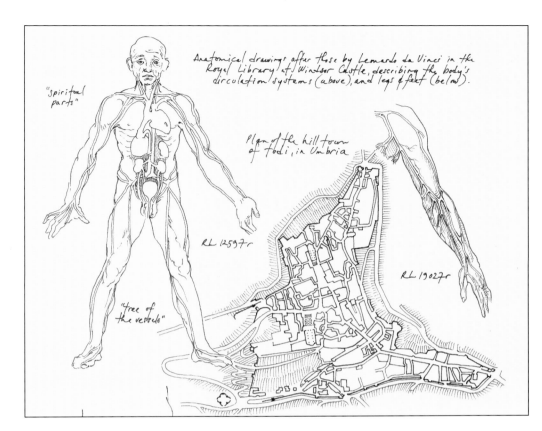

made explicit and even more meaningful by Renaissance theorists such as Francesco di Giorgio, for whom the plan of a Latin cross basilica was quite precisely and deliberately seen as representing the crucified Christ; later, Bernini would extend the image of the basilican body into his Piazza of St. Peter's, where the colonnades were seen as the "arms of the Church." The analogy could also be extended to the city at large, or at least the perfectly ordered city of the Renaissance imagination, which again explains the fascination with centralized or radial geometries.

If there was understood to be, in Renaissance humanist thought, a relationship between the body and buildings or even the city, and thus between one kind of microcosm and another kind of macrocosm, there was an even larger, more fundamental relationship understood between the body and the cosmos, and again this is the image Vitruvius wants to convey in his proportions of the ideal body. Fit within both a square

Figure 2b: *The circulation systems of the human body and medieval cities; anatomical drawings after Leonardo da Vinci. In Leonardo's drawings of the body's circulation system we can see similarities to the street networks of ancient and medieval hill towns.*

89

and a circle, the Vitruvian man mapped the order of the Ptolemaic universe onto the human form. And since this was meant to illustrate the appropriateness of the body as a model for a temple, it is no wonder Renaissance architects concluded that the most perfect temple was a centrally planned church. Thus, even though there was a less representational formal presence of the body in these buildings than there was in the basilica, one was meant to perceive a presence of the geometric structure that underlay both the individual human being and the universe. This perception could be both sensed and known, the latter the privilege of those who understood the order and causes of things.[6]

The proportions generated by the Vitruvian figure accord with the system known as *ad quadratum*, or "according to the square." While Vitruvius required a certain special pleading to make the body fit into a circle whose center is the umbilicus, there was no particular stretch required to fit the body into a square, since the height of his man is equal to the spread of his arms from fingertip to fingertip (Figure 3). The *ad quadratum* system generated an essentially modular system of proportions, or ratios dependent on multiplications of the square (1:1, 1:2, 2:3, etc.). The modular system was notably exploited by the sculptor-turned-architect Filippo Brunelleschi, whose churches especially display their modularity in the marching bays of their naves and the grids literally drawn on the floor. But there was a medieval tradition called *ad triangulum*, or "according to the triangle," which, as the modern master carpenter Stephen Finney explains, is nested within the circle in a pattern known as the "daisy wheel," and the equilateral triangles this manipulation of the radius generates served to proportion spaces vertically (especially the naves of churches), determine the pitches of roofs north of the Alps, and establish the bracing of timber framing (Figure 4). It has rarely been shown, although no doubt it was intuitively known, that this system could also be reconciled with a body inscribed within the circle. This body implicit in the triangle-within-circle would seem to have appealed later to Borromini in his designs of the remarkable Roman churches of S. Carlino and S. Ivo.

To conclude this brief excursus through the world of traditional geometry, it should be noted that the structure of the cosmos, organized around the circle, meant that to tune the body to the Harmony of the

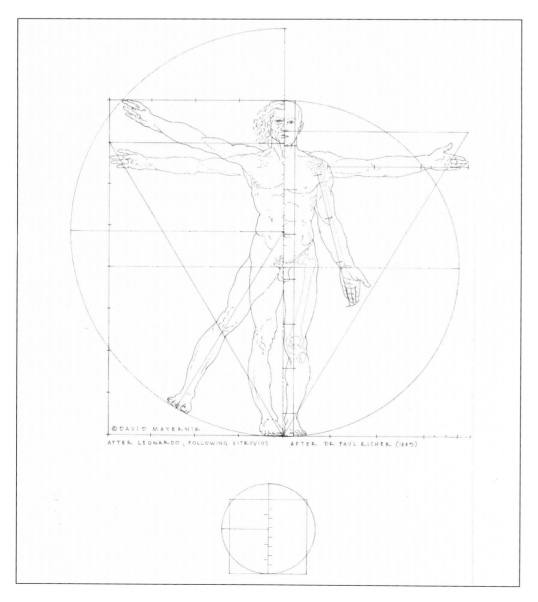

AFTER LEONARDO, FOLLOWING VITRUVIUS   AFTER DR. PAUL RICHER (1889)

©DAVID MAYERNIK

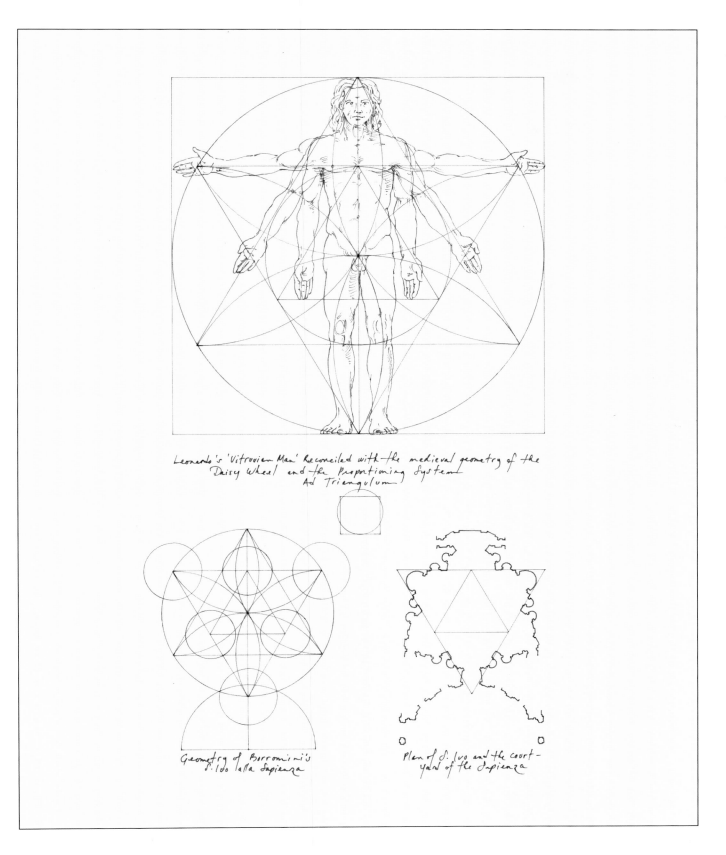

Leonardo's 'Vitruvian Man' Reconciled with the medieval geometry of the Daisy Wheel and the Proportioning System Ad Triangulum

Geometry of Borromini's S. Ido alla Sapienza

Plan of S. Ivo and the court-yard of the Sapienza

Figure 4: *Ad triangulum proportions and S. Ivo alla Sapienza. The medieval tradition called ad triangulum is nested within the circle in a pattern known as the daisy wheel, and the equilateral triangles this manipulation of the radius generates served to proportion spaces vertically (especially the naves of churches), determine the pitches of roofs north of the Alps, and establish the bracing of timber framing.*

Above: *The Women of Karyai at the Erechtheion.*

Spheres was to cure the body of disease. Thus, sixteenth- and seventeenth-century anatomical theaters often displayed the signs of the zodiac on the ceiling above the body laid out on the table, suggesting to the students in attendance that to know the body's humors was to know how they related to the stars and planets. While we no longer believe in these connections, it must be said that the notion of the integration of the body with the larger universe yielded cultures highly attuned to their interdependence, and thus avoided pitting man against nature in destructive ways.

Of course, the classical orders provided a direct parallel between the proportions of male and female bodies and columns: Tuscan and Doric suggested masculine proportions, while Ionic, Corinthian, and Composite evoked mature or young feminine proportions. Some of these associations were more than proportional (of heads to body height, or diameter to column height). They were also representative: Vitruvius described the Ionic volute as representing hair, and the column's fluting as the folds of drapery. This could extend to specific characters or moods, as when the Renaissance mathematician Luca Pacioli claimed, "The Ionic or so-called pulvinate capital is melancholic, since it does not raise itself upwards, but makes a melancholic and mournful impression like a widow."[7] What this offered to architects was a stock set of actors, if you will, who could articulate the messages the building was meant to convey: its place in the *res publica/res privata* hierarchy; its use; its relative refinement; and the status and nature of its patron. But the analogies between the parts of an order—base, shaft, and capital—suggested more precise correspondences to the body's feet, torso, and head. In some cases bodies literally substituted for columns, as in the famous Women of Karyai at the Erechtheion, or the giants on the facade of the house of the sculptor Leone Leoni in Milan.

In the centuries between the end of the ancient classical tradition and the Renaissance, medieval stone carvers introduced historiated capitals that invested columns with other layers of allusion to the figure and allowed them to be more specifically narrative. Whether in the medieval or classical traditions, columns were evocative points of contact and meaning between people and buildings, and reinforced the sense of empathy implied by the structural elements we encountered earlier. Today, stone carvers at Lincoln Cathedral's Works Department invent new capitals in their ongoing process of maintenance, investing the venerable building with allusions to the modern world.

Returning, then, to the more practical mechanics of how the body and building intersected, we should consider the body in the way that fascinated Leonardo, that is, the body in motion. It could be argued that the most fundamental practical criterion that yielded the

Left: *Reputedly the tallest building in the world for nearly a quarter of a millennium (1300–1549), Lincoln Cathedral's own team of stonemasons and carvers maintain and restore the cathedral and Close House properties.*

Figure 5: *Léon Krier, contrast of human and mechanical mobility.*

Below: *Aerial view of the Heulebrug neighborhood, part of the city of Knokke-Heist in northern Belgium, the design of which involved Léon Krier.*

humane environments of the traditional city was walkability. Léon Krier has recovered for the new traditional city the essential relationship between the convenient five- or ten-minute walk and the scale of the neighborhood. And he has also, although it has been less consistently acknowledged, pointed out the importance of vertical walkability—the idea that there is a maximum number of floors a person is prepared to climb by stairs, and these absolutely established the scale of the pre-modern city until the invention of the elevator (Figure 5). Interestingly, this maximum number of floors (five or six, depending on whether one refers to the European or American system) more or less matches the maximum practical height of multistory bearing-wall

masonry construction. The widest application of this principle in the era immediately preceding the modern city was Paris's late-nineteenth-century boulevards, where the standard number of residential floors above the ground floor (which was dedicated to commercial uses) was generally five (with an occasional garret under the roof). Having spent a summer on the top floor of one of these very effective buildings, I can attest to this number of floors as being the very limit of reasonability.

Walking not only established scale but contributed to health, since walkability meant that people actually walked (horizontally and vertically) to most of their daily needs. There were other ways in which traditional construction contributed to healthy people, and was paralleled by durable, healthful buildings. The traditional notion was that health, and conversely disease, depended on the quality of the air. This influenced not only how air was provided to buildings (for the inhabitants, and also to help the building itself "breathe") but the very siting of buildings and cities: Alberti, for example, spends no little time describing the appropriate climate, orientation, and elevation of healthful sites for cities, and Vitruvius has a notable discussion of the properties of the various winds. Again, what is of especial interest here is the way in which the building or city was anthropomorphized, made to breathe in (and out) like we do. This tendency to anthropomorphize the built world was indeed a significant source of inspiration to the building of wonderfully humane places. And it is still relevant for the development of greenfield sites, or the rehabilitation of brownfields.

Of the other elements dealt with in building, water was a critical element that had both a positive and negative aspect. Just as people needed water to drink, buildings needed to be supplied with water (ultimately to serve the inhabitants), and so access to good-quality water was an important aspect in the siting of buildings. In certain special cases, where the local waters had

curative powers, pools and even whole buildings were created to harness this healthful resource, sometimes leading to spectacular works of architecture like Rome's Villa Giulia and its *nymphaeum*, for a pope who suffered from gout. Unhealthful waters, meanwhile, were to be avoided, and transformed into healthful waters if possible, mostly operating from the principle that, since standing water was bad, getting water to move was seen to improve its quality. Water could also be corrosive to the life of a building; thus shedding (and sometimes collecting) water was a critical generative force for traditional residential forms, from the Roman *impluvium* to the monastic cistern, and the forms of traditional details such as eaves and water tables. Evacuating dirty water was a major concern in ancient Rome, whose impressive *cloaca maxima* (great sewer) channeled water out of the city. Drains, like the famous Bocca della Verità

Left: *Evacuating dirty water was a major concern in ancient Rome, whose impressive Cloaca Maxima channeled water out of the city.*

("mouth of truth"), were often created in the forms of faces, "drinking" away the runoff from streets.

In the end, there was more than a sensitively empathetic aspect to this relationship of the small and the big, or between the body, the building, and the universe: there was also an ethical, moral, and spiritual dimension. To build in attunement with the body and the cosmos was to do good, to render the world more beautiful and useful for human flourishing:

> [A] work of art, the microcosmic reflection of the macrocosm, expresses and appeals to the most rational part of the mind, as well as to the highest emotions, and in its total effect induces in the whole soul and body that balance, harmony, and proportion the soul ideally should possess in itself, should impose on and share with the body, and should take pleasure in perceiving and receiving.[8]

Lessons for Today

What, in practical terms, does all of this traditional wisdom about bodies and buildings mean for architects and builders today? At least three essential principles can be derived from a close examination of how traditional cultures saw the body in their buildings.

First, that in order to create suitable habitations for humans, architects today need to be as familiar with the body as with buildings. The most effective way to achieve this is to develop competence in drawing the human form. This practical skill is a means of comprehending the body's nature, and facilitates the design of elegant, sustainable, humane buildings.

Second, that architecture is fundamentally for people, but people are a part of nature. Therefore the more responsive architecture is to the person, and to his or her movements, the more sympathetic architecture is to the natural world. The flaw in the modern landscape

is not an excessive focus on the human element, but rather that dependence on the man-made machine (cars, elevators, air-conditioning systems) has overridden concern for the mechanics of nature.

Third, as the human body does not fundamentally change over time—just as rain, wind, and gravity remain constant—design with and for the body establishes much of the durability of buildings, or of their long-term ability to satisfy the human mind, body, and soul. The size, needs, and limitations of the body establish sustainable parameters for building across cultures and times. These are not arcane references to defunct cultural constructs, but commonsense truths about building well and durably. Beyond the practically useful aspects of accommodating the built world to human needs, buildings built with us in mind, so to speak, generate an environment that is inherently appealing, places where we can feel at home, a meaningful world of beauty and balance.

A selection of modern applications of these principles can serve as hopeful signs that we are recovering our common sense in building. In my own work I have striven to introduce traditional references to the body into buildings as diverse as a gymnasium and a library, not to mention larger-scale master planning. Other architects and craftspeople who are attuned to these same issues, even when not explicitly introducing anthropomorphic references into their projects, operate according to these venerable principles. The projects illustrated here offer some ways in which buildings and bodies can constructively inform each other again today.

Master carpenter Stephen Finney is one of few people today who has built two traditional working windmills. Finney has taught in the Prince's Foundation Building Crafts Apprentices program, and advocates the use of traditional dimensioning systems like the rod (sixteen feet, six inches or three people each five feet six inches tall) and the geometric figure of the daisy wheel

"At least three essential principles can be derived from a close examination of how traditional cultures saw the body in their buildings."

(with the *ad triangulum* proportions it generates) in the layout of modern timber framing. With ample evidence of its use in medieval construction (where it can be seen inscribed on the timbers of Lincoln Cathedral's roof, for example), his geometric method of proportioning and traditional units of measure suggest that if we want to generate results as successful as those of the great buildings of the past, we do well to employ their methodologies. Apart from revivifying our traditions, the advantages of the daisy-wheel technique of arriving at proportions are that it is scalable, low-tech, and integrated. Being scalable, it is applicable from the

Below: *Model of a timber building proportioned ad triangulum. Master carpenter Stephen Finney advocates the use of traditional dimensioning systems such as the rod and the daisy wheel.*

smallest elements of a building to its overall proportions. This is partially accomplished by the way its larger scale is achieved by modularity, multiplying small modules to generate larger ones. And, of course, the same logic obtains in scaling up from a small model to actual construction. Being low-tech, it is both easily learnable and translatable to any economic strata of construction. And being integrated means it simultaneously, and therefore comprehensively, describes a system of proportions for plans, sections, and construction details.

Implicit in this technique is the figure of a body, not dissimilar to Vitruvius' ideal man. The body, therefore, is nested in the overall design—and specific detailing—of buildings rooted in this system, contributing to our sense of empathy with our environment. It is the simplicity and common sense of this method that recommends it as a strategy for determining parameters for a sensible environment. Moreover, advocating artisanal heavy-timber (as opposed to industrial lightweight balloon-frame) construction establishes a value for higher initial cost but long-term durability, instead of short-term cost-effectiveness and long-term unsustainability. This privileging of durability over throwaway construction is especially critical for our public realm, where our shared values are manifested and our commitment to continuity is most critical.

Architect Thomas N. Rajkovich's design for a market loggia for Evanston, Illinois (Figure 6), is rooted in a humanist understanding of the rapport between construction and representation, and of the integration of classical *ad quadratum* proportions with classical building. Leon Battista Alberti titled his treatise on architecture *The Art of Building* (*De Re Ædificatoria*), but Rajkovich believes we can no longer assume that today's building construes building well as it did in the fifteenth century. His loggia, then, is a polemical proposition illustrating *The Art of Proper Building* (*Ars Recte*

> **"We live in a world in which most buildings have expected life spans measured in decades, not centuries, meaning we are building a throw-away landscape by the standards of pre-modern culture."**

Ædificandi): it demonstrates not only the tectonic relationship between construction and language (in, for example, the ways his timber trusses shape eaves that imply a classical stone entablature), but also the virtues of stability and durability, the proper concerns of building well. These things cannot be taken for granted. We live in a world in which most buildings have expected life spans measured in decades, not centuries, meaning we are building a throwaway landscape by the standards of pre-modern culture. But by throwaway I do not mean degradable: the materials with which we build are often not only nonbiodegradable but also toxic, so that when they are thrown away, they pose just as great a threat to our environment as they did when they were standing. Building well, then, means building with materials with low-embodied energy, and building at once durably and yet with naturally degradable or reusable materials. Timber and stone in fact satisfy all three criteria.

There is in this loggia an implicit constructive ethos and an explicit constructive aesthetic. As Rajkovich writes (in correspondence with the author), "The artistic intervention which separates the ideal/representational from the real/necessary, and which distinguishes architecture from building, is rendered evident in each element of the design." Building becomes architecture in rendering poetic what is necessary. Part of the poetics comes from a harkening back to the origins of stone architecture in primitive wood construction; in other words, Rajkovich's approach to architecture is as much anthropological as anthropomorphic, in that it consciously roots how we build today in how we began building. This is another form of intuitive or empathetic understanding that the traditional approach to building offers to its audience: a belief that we recognize (consciously or unconsciously), and naturally appreciate, our ancestral ways of making.

But Rajkovich's proposition does not stop at the constructive: he has invested this useful civic building

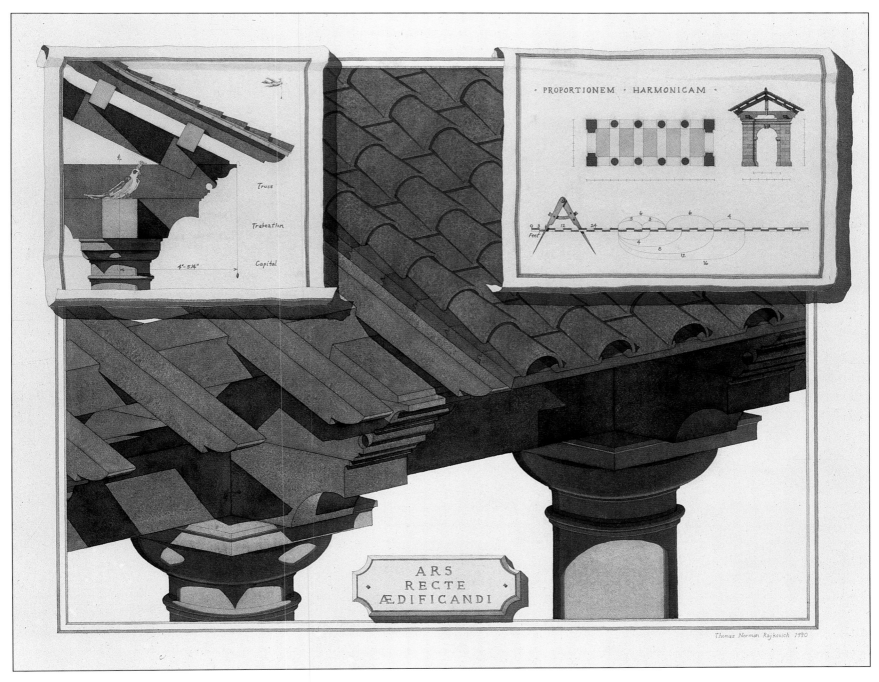

with humanist principles of proportion and harmony. The proportions of the loggia in plan, section, and elevation are regulated by harmonic consonances: octaves, fifths, and fourths, in ratios of 1:2, 2:3, and 3:4. By thinking of them harmonically, he recalls the traditional rapport between music and architecture, or the idea that we sense, both aurally and visually, these simple ratios as being inherently beautiful (whether or not they are in accordance with the Harmony of the Spheres). Part of the perception of musical analogies—octaves, rhythm, tempo—in architecture is also conveyed by its tectonic elements: the disposition of columns and

Figure 6: *Architect Thomas N. Rajkovich's design for a market loggia for Evanston, Illinois.*

walls march out easily recognized figurative elements that we intuitively measure or count. The market loggia begins and ends its composition with two walls framing four Tuscan columns on each side. The walls' corners function also as piers that mediate the transition of the system from mural to columnar. In the disposition of elements and in their relationship—how columns and walls interact being a key component of the rhetoric of the classical language—this way of building offers an elegantly logical system that extends from constructive elements to buildings to groupings of buildings into villages and cities. According the parts to the whole is one of the fundamental lessons derived from drawing the human body, and in classical building it orchestrates everything from architectural details to compositions at the urban scale.

The design and grouping of buildings on boarding school campuses can be seen as a metaphor of the school community itself, where unique individuals also have a collective identity—ideally one organized around

Below: *Rajkovich's proposition does not stop at the constructive; he has invested this useful civic building with humanist principles of proportion and harmony.*

an ethos about education of the whole person toward future citizenship. The gymnasium is the first phase of our master plan for the TASIS campus on the hills above Lugano, Switzerland; it is a key component of the campus' "Global Village" idea (since its students typically represent over forty different countries), and is the school's largest building. Planning the campus as a village, both to create a greater sense of community and to preserve the maximum amount of open green space, means that each building takes on a unique role in the campus' *res publica*. The gymnasium in particular has a pivotal role to play in the life of the school, providing athletic, performance, and educational facilities; in that sense it contributes to shaping both body and mind. Its form and character are responses to its urban and educational functions, are signs of its civic

role, and are rooted in the very origins of the words *gymnasium* and *palestra*.

The idea or *concetto* for the form of the gymnasium emerged from a Renaissance project by Pirro Ligorio for the courtyard of the Roman university, the Sapienza: Ligorio's unfinished project for a double-apsed space was meant to be his reconstruction of the plan of an ancient Greek gymnasium (actually, it more resembled the form of the outdoor *palestræ* of Roman baths). For the TASIS gymnasium, the apses also provide practical extra space where the players need it the most, behind the baskets, and modulate the scale of the front facade of the building with their lower roofs.

The second-floor *palestra* space itself is naturally ventilated, a working body that can breathe. The structure uses reinforced traditional masonry bearing-

Above: *The gymnasium is the first phase of the master plan for the TASIS campus in the hills above Lugano, Switzerland; it is a key component of the campus' "Global Village" idea.*

101

Right: *Views of the TASIS gymnasium.*

Left: *The Lisbon waterfront master plan in the form of a traditional azulejo tile wall.*

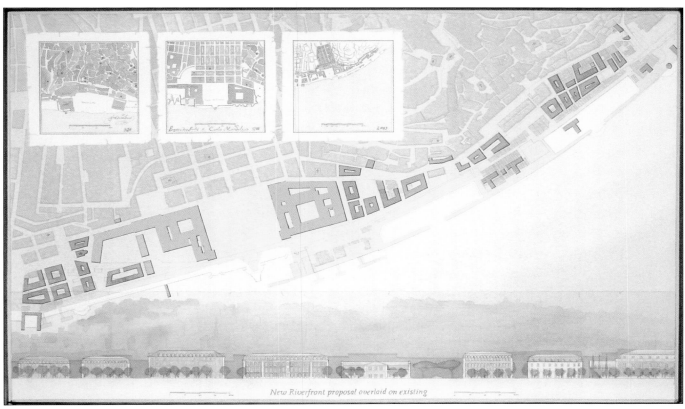

New Riverfront proposal overlaid on existing

Left: *Plan of the Lisbon Waterfront, including diagrams of its historical evolution, and elevation of the city toward the Tagus River. Gonçalo Cornelio da Silva's project for the Lisbon waterfront is at once a realistic and a visionary proposal, addressing modern issues of regional multimodal transportation while projecting a timeless, humane civic image to the wider world.*

Right: *Plan and section of the Praça do Comercio.*

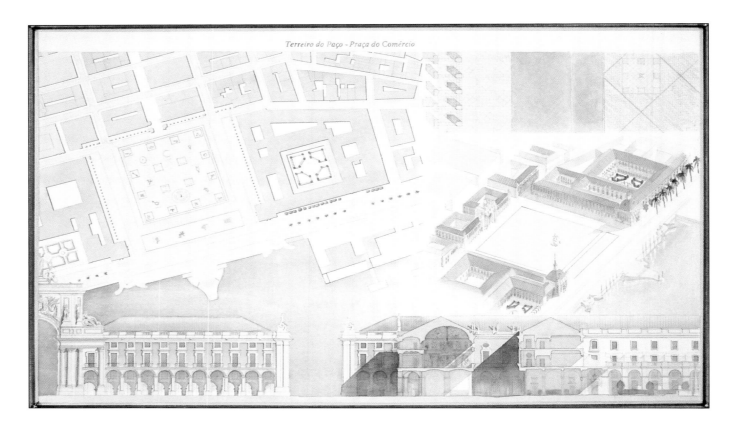

Right: *Area plan and elevation of the Praça toward the river.*

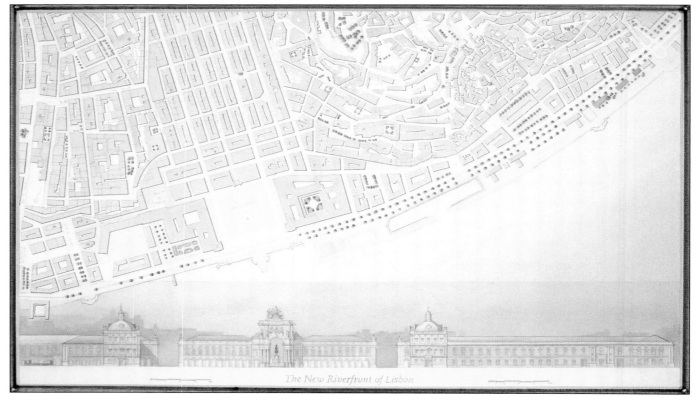

of the Tagus restores a human and civic dimension to this great maritime city, not unlike Venice's presentation of herself at the Piazzetta di San Marco. The fabric that then frames the historic Praça finally allows the great space to be read as an event in a denser matrix rather than as an undifferentiated open space flanked by even less well-defined spaces. It extends the Praça's arms east and west to embrace the whole of the riverfront.

The humanist conception of history that this project represents—that we are continually in the process of "completing" the historical narrative—balances continuity with innovation, perhaps the only sane approach to urban interventions. The stuff of which da Silva's urban fabric is made subsumes all of the body references we have noted historically: a "healthy" distribution of movement systems (people, trolleys, trains, buses, boats); classically anthropomorphic buildings; restoration of a primary urban space that bodily embraces citizens and visitors alike; and symbolic cues in the plaza's paving that speak to our relationship to the cosmos (the planetary signs and the Four Elements). It is a microcosm, whether of the developed world or the cosmos itself, and a macrocosm of the individual body. At once bold and discreet, the desire for urban wholeness that this project represents is a significant consequence of a body-oriented approach to urban design.

Cities and Landscapes are the tangible expression[s] of our material & spiritual worth. For good or ill they express and define how we use or waste our resources, energy, time, and land. . . . So far Washington's monumental core is but an outline sketch of a great city to be, a grand skeleton with noble limbs but little flesh. In those hundreds of empty acres I see but an unfinished canvas, an incomplete portrait which craves for completion.

—Léon Krier, dedicatory inscription to his master plan for Washington, D.C.[9]

Léon Krier's plan for Washington starts from the premise that L'Enfant's plan established the bones of a great city, but the flesh was lacking; in other words, that the networks of streets and distribution of monumental buildings describe an armature upon which a great city could be, but has not yet been, built. In Krier's analysis, the extensive armature itself needs to be clarified into discrete "towns" and enriched by a finer grain of texture, of more fabric between the monuments, and a greater overall clarity in its juxtaposition of the natural and the man-made. In that sense he restores an organic sensibility to the complex system that is a great city. But more fundamentally, he addresses a critical challenge of D.C.'s plan. L'Enfant enabled, if he did not intentionally design, a city that facilitates the machine; in other words, with its

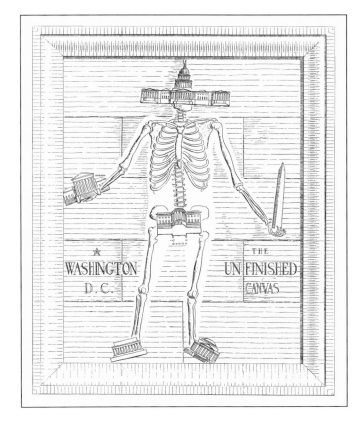

Left: Washington, D.C.: The Unfinished Canvas. *Léon Krier's plan for Washington starts from the premise that L'Enfant's plan established the bones of a great city, but the flesh was lacking.*

Right: *Léon Krier,* An Anti-City of Functional Zones vs. A City of Urban Communities.

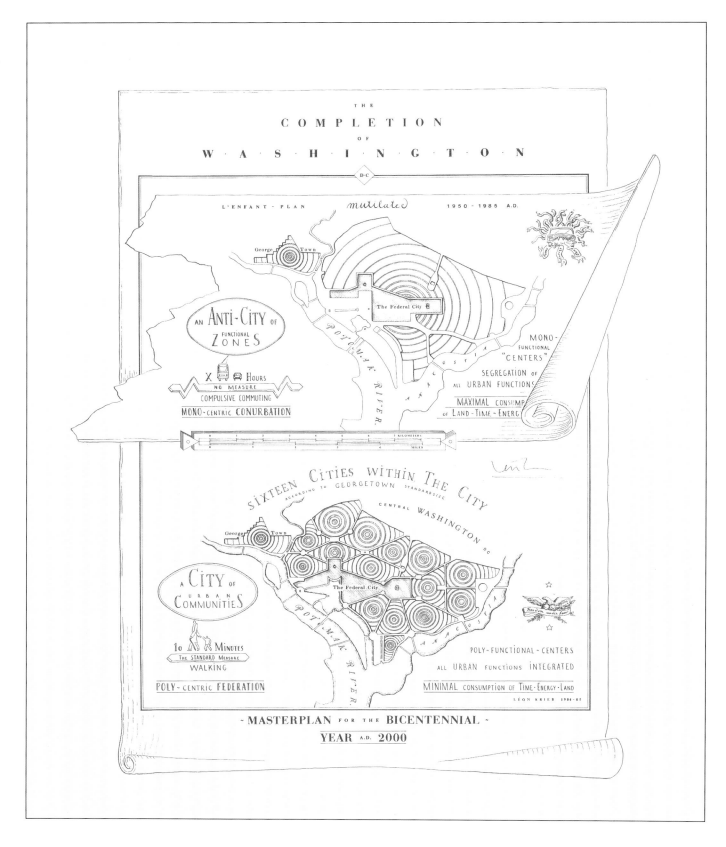

long, wide boulevards, L'Enfant's Washington plan is a mechanistic city *avant la machine*. To be clear, it is not that L'Enfant intended this, but that his inevitable dependence on carriages and horses for the connections he made across miles of erstwhile marshland translated all too easily into a car-dependent city. Krier, then, doesn't actually restore the human dimension to Washington's streets and public spaces; he courageously imposes it on a plan within which they were too easily sacrificed. This explains, too, the most controversial part of his plan—turning the western half of the Mall into a Venice-inspired lagoon. In Krier's walkable, body-oriented city,

the current Mall is far too vast to be a properly urban space, and so it makes sense to return part of it to nature (recalling the original condition of the Potomac plain). This move needs to be understood, too, in the context of a sequence of spaces that culminates in the *place civique* (Constitution Square), which he proposes in front of the Capitol: a truly urban, human-scaled space, albeit rather grand by his pre-modern European standards, that stands in poignant contrast to his lagoon. This could only be anachronistic if juxtaposed to the sweep of the Mall today—which is, again, neither a properly urban nor truly natural environment.

Above: *Léon Krier, view of the proposed Grand Canal.*

109

The key to Krier's way of thinking is the notion that good cities are composed of smaller units, which can be defined as neighborhoods and towns. In redefining Washington with reference to Georgetown, he is actually elaborating on a de facto compartmentalization of the District of Columbia created in large part by the rupture that is the Mall. His Lincoln-Town, Washington-Town, Jefferson-Town, and Capitol-Town revolve clockwise around his reduced Mall and its monuments, giving to Washington some of the structure of London, which has been assembled over time out of a series of discrete towns and villages. Perhaps not coincidentally, Krier was living in London when he designed the project for Washington.

The human scale that Léon Krier restores to Washington operates at the level of the grand civic plan, but also at the individual block level. In Lincoln-Town, for example, he offers a residential block type with street walls and gardens between three- and four-story buildings. Not only do these typologies offer variety to the street but they also install residential units in otherwise mono-functional, institutional districts—a key element in making any city humane and livable. This

Below: *Léon Krier, view of the proposed Constitution Square.*

strategy, of all the elements of Krier's visionary plan, is the one that is most desperately needed in a city that in the last two decades has lurched toward a more integrated urban fabric but has sacrificed human scale to maximum developer build-outs.

What these projects represent is a recovery of an intuitive wisdom about building the world in harmony with nature, a wisdom that we largely lost in the twentieth century. While we have experienced progress in so many areas of human endeavor, from political liberties to medicine, we have mostly witnessed a precipitous decline in the quality of our built landscape. That intuitive wisdom, which is inevitably cross-cultural—as it speaks to the constants of our bodies and the natural world in all their variety—is also cultural: it was made poetic (by Homer), rational (by Leonardo), and invested with wider significance (by Vitruvius) over millennia of practice and reflection. At the same time, it was not stylistically prescriptive but rather allowed latitude for the evolution of architectural language.

Reestablishing the body as a paradigm for buildings and cities is one of the most effective ways of restoring balance to the built and natural landscapes, and to culture itself. Perhaps, then, these challenging times can be a hopeful point of departure for a recovery of the best of our classical traditions: Responding to the current crisis of our impact on the world may actually hold the potential for building not only a healthier environment but a more humane civilization.

Notes to Chapter 6

[1] Alberto Pérez Gomez, *Architecture and the Crisis of Modern Science* (Cambridge, Mass.: MIT Press, 1990), p.207.

[2] Homer, *The Iliad*, 23: 791–94, trans. Robert Fagles (New York: Penguin, 1991), p. 581.

[3] Leon Battista Alberti, *On the Art of Building in Ten Books*, trans. Rykwert et al. (Cambridge, Mass.: MIT Press, 1991), III, pp. 85–86.

[4] Pietro Aretino, letter to Andrea Udone, translated in John Onians, *Bearers of Meaning* (Princeton, N.J.: Princeton University Press, 1989), p. 299.

[5] Richard Sennett, *Flesh and Stone: The Body and the City in Western Civilization* (New York: W. W. Norton, 1994), p. 270.

[6] *"While listening, we perceive with our senses the concordant parts; we measure the intervals and concordances with our reason and with the help of our musical training. . . . On account of this we are entitled to call our soul reasonable: viz, because it is a measuring and numbering power which grasps whatever requires precise distinction. . . . Thus reason, seeing that concord is based on number and proportion, invented the rational theory of musical chords, based on the theory of numbers."* Nicholas of Cusa, *De ludo globi*, lib. II, translated in Kathi Meyer-Baer, "Nicholas of Cusa on the Meaning of Music," *The Journal of Aesthetics and Art Criticism* (Philadelphia: Blackwell Publishing, June 1947) p. 304.

[7] *De divina proportione*, 1509, trans. John Onians, *Bearers of Meaning*, p. 221.

[8] H. James Jensen, *The Muses' Concord: Literature, Music, and the Visual Arts in the Baroque Age* (Bloomington: Indiana University Press, 1976), p. 3.

[9] In *Archives d'Architecture Moderne*, 1986.

Sustainable Refurbishment:

A Key Component of the Built Heritage

Dr. Tim Yates

> *" The establishment of larger communities of people provided a critical mass of workers with sufficient time to specialize in aspects of craft; later, people were needed to labor within the industrial economy, which proved to be a way of providing the houses and workplaces of the workers and of attracting an even greater number to the promise of wealth. "*

There is today a renewed interest in the refurbishment of domestic and nondomestic buildings in response to the requirement both to improve the living conditions in many older houses and to reduce the emission of greenhouse gases. It is estimated that in the U.K. alone about 4.2 million houses date from before 1919 and are in need of refurbishment and upgrading. In addition, there are another 2 million houses dating from after 1919 that fall below the level of what are considered to be "decent homes."

The total investment required both to improve living conditions and to reduce energy consumption by 60 percent in these houses is in the order of £100 billion at present costs. Because refurbishment is an essential component of maintaining our urban landscape and sustaining our communities, the investment must be made. However, it must be made in such a way that the techniques and materials used blend innovation and tradition in order to minimize environmental impact while maximizing effectiveness.

Urbanization is part of our world. Our urban areas have grown from small beginnings in the Near East some ten thousand years ago to dominate our world and provide the environment in which a considerable proportion of the world's population lives today. The establishment of larger communities of people provided a critical mass of workers with sufficient time to specialize in aspects of craft; later, people were needed to labor within the industrial economy, which proved to be a way of providing the houses and workplaces of the workers and of attracting an even greater number to the promise of wealth. This phase now seems to have passed in Europe and North America—the "Global North"—but remains true in the "Global South."

In the Global North we now see ourselves as being in a postindustrial period, and so what we expect and demand from our urban areas has also changed. The decline in heavy industry was paralleled by a decline in investment by local and national governments and by individuals who no longer had the ability or incentive to invest as employment dropped in many traditional industries in our urban areas. In the United Kingdom this trend was particularly apparent in the north of England, South Wales, and the central belt of Scotland. In the United States similar declines in traditional industries have been seen in cities such as Pittsburgh and Detroit. The decline in heavy industries has been followed by increasing urban deprivation, lack of employment, and depressed economies.

To break the spiral of increasing deprivation, programs of renewal and regeneration were, and still are, needed, and these require investing time and money. The scale of the problem was such that some saw the only way forward as large-scale clearance followed by a rebuilding

Left: *Ruins of the Packard Motor Car Company's factory in Detroit. The plant was designed by Albert Kahn in 1907 and was the first to use reinforced concrete. At one point, Packard was the biggest-selling luxury car in the United States.*

the infrastructure, housing, and local economies. And of necessity this rebuilding involved the destruction and "regeneration" of local communities that had developed over many years. In many places social needs took second place to the demands of economics—perhaps a reflection of the extent of the social problems in some areas, which had their origins in the lack of investment and neglect.

It was inevitable that the lack of investment and reduction in employment would result in urban decline and eventually the failure of the housing market, with supply outstripping demand. G. Bramley and H. Pawson suggest that low-demand localities can be divided into three broad groups.[1] In the first there is a low demand across all tenures, generally of a serious magnitude and impact. In the second there is low demand or oversupply of social housing—rental or shared-ownership housing provided by government or housing associations—accompanied by adequate or buoyant private market conditions. In the third there are isolated patches of unpopular social housing in generally high-demand areas.

Although these groups can largely be defined by factual data, the causes of each situation are harder to determine and deal with. P. Keenan writes that low-demand areas are characterized by the abandonment of dwellings and, often, whole neighborhoods:

Abandonment of property is the process by which residential units . . . become detached from the housing market in a number of ways and eventually fall into disuse, in effect abandoned by their owners.[2]

Once abandoned, the houses either fall into a state of complete disrepair or are occupied by unofficial, transient tenants. The properties affected are in both public and private sectors (including housing association dwellings), range across all tenures, and include properties that are in good condition and even some that are newly constructed and have never been occupied.

Keenan contends that abandoned properties are a waste of resources, and a major factor contributing to the downward spiral of some inner cities, emptying neighborhoods of social and economic activity.

The appearance of one or two abandoned properties appear to be sufficient to trigger what seemed like a virus, attaching randomly in clearly defined and weakened neighbourhoods.[3]

Keenan *et al.* discuss literature from the U.S. that postulates that the root of the problem is the decline and collapse of major industrial sectors. Literature from the U.K. on this topic is more difficult to find, and typically focuses on "voids" and "vacants"—terms commonly used in the social housing sector. Keenan says the main causes of abandonment are: the depopulation of large cities and loss of manufacturing jobs; a chronic mismatch of supply and demand at the local level; the unpopularity of neighborhoods with poor housing or high crime; and a rapid increase in the number of low-demand or abandoned dwellings. Thus, while the symptom is the abandoned dwellings, the causes are social in origin. To what extent, then, will dealing with the symptoms (by refurbishing or replacing the existing housing stock) solve the problem? This is a major issue in government policy related to the regeneration and renewal of buildings and communities.

Meeting the Needs of the People

A celebrated paper on human motivation, written by Abraham Maslow in 1943, has become one of the classic works on the needs of organisms, including mankind.[4] In the paper Maslow defines a "five-stage" hierarchy of needs (Figure 1) that postulates that we must satisfy each need in turn, starting with the first and most obvious need for survival itself. Only when the lower-order needs of physical and emotional well-being are satisfied are we concerned with the higher-order needs of influence and personal development. At the base of this hierarchy are the physiological needs of eating, drinking, sleeping, and reproduction. If these are not fulfilled, they take priority, and can control thoughts and behaviors.

The second level includes the need for safety—personal security as regards crime, health, and well-being—which emerges only after the previous needs are filled. The third level of human needs is social, and includes emotion-based relationships in general, such as friendship and family, and the need to feel a sense of belonging and acceptance by a larger social group or community.

Figure 1: *Maslow's Hierarchy of Needs—original five-stage model.*

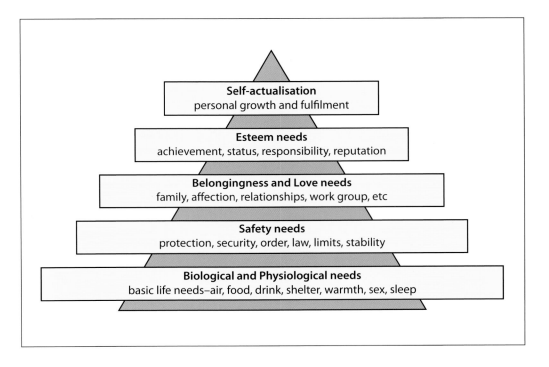

Maslow argues that only after these three levels of needs are met can humans become interested in learning, exploration, discovery, and creativity in order to gain better understanding of the world around them, and the aesthetic need for beauty. If these needs are met, it becomes possible to attain self-actualization.

If we consider this hierarchy correct, then we can see that to regenerate communities and renew urban areas we must be able to provide houses that meet the basic physiological and safety needs: a dry, warm, and safe place in which to live. Simultaneously, we need to provide urban areas where communities can be reestablished so as to meet social needs.

Sustainable Housing and Sustainable Communities

The Sustainable Communities Plan issued by the U.K. government in 2003 defines sustainable housing as:

> . . . housing that meets the perceived and real needs of the present in a resource efficient fashion, whilst providing attractive, safe and ecologically rich neighbourhoods.[5]

This definition can be applied equally well to new build and to refurbishment. There is indeed a renewed emphasis in favor of the retention of existing buildings, except in cases where it can be demonstrated that the overall housing market can be improved by the removal of a limited number of houses—if, for example, there is a housing surplus or a need to create open space to enhance the overall environment.

Thinking about regeneration and sustainability has evolved over the last ten years. The goal is no longer simply to reduce energy consumption; the needs of the people who occupy, or who will occupy, the refurbished houses must be taken into account, as well as the

economic and social revival of a location. There is a renewed interest in the value that people ascribe to places—which goes far beyond their economic value. The term value here includes (adapted from *Conservation Principles for the Sustainable Management of the Historic Environment*, English Heritage, 2005):

Aesthetic Value: Relating to the ways in which people respond to a place through sensory and intellectual experience of it;

Community Value: Relating to the meanings of a place for the people who identify with it, and whose collective memory it holds;

Evidential Value: Relating to the potential of a place to yield primary information about past human activity;

Historical Value: Relating to the ways in which a place can provide direct links to past people, events, and aspects of life;

Instrumental Value: Economic, educational, recreational, and other benefits that exist as a consequence of the cultural or natural heritage values of a place.

The introduction to the International Committee on Monuments and Sites (ICOMOS) "Charter on the Built Vernacular Heritage" in 1999 states:

> The built vernacular heritage occupies a central place in the affection and pride of all people. . . . Although it is the work of man it is also the creation of time. It would be unworthy of the heritage of man if care were not taken to conserve these traditional harmonies which constitute the core of man's own existence. The built vernacular heritage is important; it is the fundamental expression of the culture of a community, of its

" To regenerate communities and renew urban areas we must be able to provide houses that meet the basic physiological and safety needs: a dry, warm, and safe place in which to live. "

relationship with its territory and, at the same time, the expression of the world's cultural diversity.[6]

This statement reinforces the link between the needs of people and the expression of community seen in the built environment. It also provides a strong social argument in favor of the retention of buildings, which in turn supports the arguments for retaining buildings in order to avoid the waste of natural resources.

However, it is accepted that there must be a sustainability limit that is a complex interaction of social and environmental needs, as well as economics. The needs and wishes of society, particularly those most closely associated with a building or its immediate environs, could result in what is perceived as an unacceptable environmental impact—the creation of additional parking spaces at the expense of existing open spaces or habitats, for example. But it is more likely that the limit will be financial—that is, the

amount of investment required to achieve an improvement in energy efficiency or the standard of housing cannot be justified in terms of the likely returns. This is often a problem when demand for this type of housing is limited and unemployment or social deprivation is high.

The Nelson Housing Market Regeneration Scheme

Nelson, Lancashire, has many shops and businesses and is the seat of the local council. It was formed by the combination of two villages, Great and Little Marsden, in the early nineteenth century, and the new community grew rapidly as a textile mill town. The challenges that housing market renewal in Nelson needed to address included an oversupply of terraced houses, often smaller than required by many local families; a backlog of investment in housing that was leading to a high number of "unfit" properties; the deterioration of conditions within residential neighborhoods and the town center, and a lack of facilities; poor private-sector landlords;

Left: *View of the Whitefield area of Nelson, Lancashire, U.K. St. Mary's Church is on the right and the Leeds–Liverpool Canal and M65 motorway are in the foreground.*

Above: *Terrace of houses refurbished as part of the St. Mary's Conservation Scheme.*

low-quality employment opportunities; and poor educational attainment. All are aspects of the cycle of poverty, from which it is difficult to break free.

A public inquiry was held in January 2002 over Pendle Borough Council's plan to declare a clearance area in the Whitefield district of Nelson. The proposals included the purchase, demolition, and redevelopment of 160 Victorian mill-worker houses. The inquiry found in favor of the retention of the houses, but the Office of the Deputy Prime Minister asked for it to be reopened in 2003 to consider whether retention was still viable in the current housing market. The inquiry again found in favor and a new plan was developed. In 2004 the Prince's Foundation for the Built Environment held an Enquiry by Design to provide a forum for consultations with stakeholders.

Out of these discussions, four priority action areas were identified, including the Whitefield area and the town center. In November 2005 the Whitefield

Regeneration Partnership, composed of agencies, heritage organizations, and local residents, was established to coordinate activities and oversee improvements. There were proposals to bring more than one hundred empty houses back into use through refurbishment and imaginative conversions of two properties into one—a choice popular with residents in an area where there are many extended families—and to build more than eighty new homes. Both new and refurbished homes were to be green and energy efficient with average fuel bills of less than £50 per year. There were also plans to provide a range of new community facilities for all of Nelson, including a new community center, to create a major public square as the focus of the new community, and to reconnect Whitefield with the center of Nelson, the canal, and the surrounding landscape.

In the St. Mary's conservation area of Nelson, a £3.9-million group repair scheme has been completed with

Below: *A view along Every Street showing the stark contrast between the refurbished houses (on the right) and the adjacent streets.*

funding from the Elevate Housing Market Renewal Scheme. Elevate East Lancashire is one of the U.K. government's nine housing-market renewal agencies charged with finding innovative solutions to the problem of low demand, negative equity, and housing-market collapse.

Most of the properties were in private ownership and occupied at the time, and the emphasis was on regenerating the external fabric. The scheme included fitting traditional double-glazed sash windows to improve energy efficiency, re-laying the roofs, and insulating the roof spaces. The work was to use traditional materials and to retain original design features for the chimney stacks in keeping with the period of the homes. In addition, plans included the replacement of front doors and rainwater goods, the cleaning and repointing of external masonry, and the refurbishment of boundary walls and gates to improve the overall appearance. In some houses limited work, including the replacement of rotten floor joists, to cite one example, was carried out internally.

A total of 180 properties were scheduled for improvement, but there was funding only for about 120 houses.

Below: *Terrace of seven houses being refurbished by Adactus in Every Street, Nelson.*

As it was a market-renewal scheme, the goal was to have a positive impact on the area as a whole by stimulating the housing market and drawing in further private investment. The cost of the work varied between £28,000 and £32,000 per house (in 2006 prices), depending on the extent of the work.

The available data suggest that the investment has in general been successful in financial terms, as the sale prices recorded from 2004 to 2006 show an increase from about £25,000 for a two-bedroom house prior to refurbishment to about £55,000 afterward. Properties originally scheduled for demolition have a much lower market value—about £10,000–15,000—but need considerably more work to bring them up to standard.

This approach to renewal has had a significant effect on the appearance of the houses and their external envelope, and assumes that a more buoyant housing market will result in greater investment by owners inside their houses—for example, on appliances and more efficient central heating systems—and by the local authority in the neighborhood. The refurbishment scheme enabled the retention of many of the original features of the houses and maintained the appearance of the streetscape within the conservation area.

Elsewhere in Nelson, the Adactus Housing Association refurbished a short terrace of houses on Every Street to show how old houses can be given a new inside layout and design to suit modern living. Adactus bought seven houses from Pendle Council for £1 and created two houses with three bedrooms by knocking two houses together at each end of the terrace, as well as three single-bedroom units in the remaining three homes. Work started in April 2006 and was completed early in 2007.

The work was far more extensive than for the St. Mary's conservation area project, and allowed for greater improvements in the thermal performance and efficiency of the fixtures and fittings. It was hoped that a program of guidance and education on policies and actions, as part of a wider scheme for house owners in the area, would improve sustainability. The negative side was a reduction in the reuse of materials as a result of the more extensive remodeling of each property, unless a plan for the salvaging and reuse of the materials had been previously implemented. There was far less potential here for the retention of the original features of the houses—though the streetscape remained largely unaltered.

The two projects in Nelson demonstrated that the current housing stock in the Whitefield area is extremely adaptable and can be refurbished to a standard that makes the project economically viable. The more extensive refurbishment along Every Street has the potential to provide very energy-efficient houses with interesting internal spaces. But this produces significant amounts of waste and requires an extensive use of modern materials with a potentially high environmental impact.

However, it is possible to envision two approaches that could reduce the environmental impact while maintaining a more conservation-based approach. The first is to consider the use of a district heating system based on a bio-mass boiler, which would be carbon neutral or very close to neutral even if the individual houses were not insulated to the highest standards. The installation of a district heating system would require changes in the infrastructure, but if this were undertaken as part of the overall regeneration it would be less difficult. The potential environmental impact could be further reduced by combining the use of carbon-neutral technology with the reuse of construction materials, supplemented by low-environmental-impact traditional materials such as lime mortars and insulation made from sheep's wool, newspaper, and timber.

The Whitefield Housing Market Renewal scheme has since received permission to refurbish 211 more properties.

" There is indeed a renewed emphasis in favor of the retention of existing buildings."

121

Right: *Franklin Boulevard Historic District, Pontiac, Michigan.*

Pontiac, Michigan

There are many similar regeneration projects in the U.S., including the celebrated regeneration and restoration of brownstone houses in New York[7] and the preservation and improvement of historic homes in Savannah, Georgia. One of the best-documented schemes is the regeneration of Pontiac, Michigan, which has a population of 67,124 and is an urban center with a significant manufacturing sector, surrounded by affluent metropolitan Detroit suburbs. Pontiac grew rapidly and by the early twentieth century was a major center for the production of cars, trucks, and buses. But as in so many cities in late-twentieth-century Michigan, Pontiac suffered from changes in retailing and the automotive industry, an eroding tax base, racial strife, and economic recession—all of which contributed to a serious decline in economic activity. The 2000 census showed that about 18 percent of families and 22.1 percent of the population lived below the poverty line, including 29.3 percent of those under age eighteen.

In 2003 the Pontiac Development Initiative Report stated that:

Although located in one of the most affluent counties in the United States, Pontiac found itself in decline relative to its suburban neighbors. In the past, Pontiac tried every new development strategy— large catalyst projects, Urban Renewal demolition and land assembly, transportation beltways, entertainment and arts districts—all designed to revitalize an urban core. With so much focus and expenditures in the downtown area, neighborhoods felt that they were not receiving the attention they needed to maintain and increase in value. Private real estate developers and businesses began to think that there were too many barriers to development and too few incentives to stay in Pontiac.[8]

The mayor and the city council developed a strategy to address the problems in a holistic way, including both downtown and neighborhood revitalization, starting with existing assets—including the remaining cultural institutions and important businesses. The aim of the Pontiac Preservation Development Initiative (PDI) was to create an economically strong and physically attractive city.

The work began with development of a strategy to preserve the city's historic and conservation districts, recognizing that these could serve as the basis for economic development and result in improvement of the overall built environment—in social and environmental terms, as well as economically. The plan was based on a comprehensive preservation assessment conducted by the National Trust for Historic Preservation, with the goal of making recommendations to the city that would prioritize preservation as a community and economic development strategy. The assessment focused on downtown and neighborhood revitalization, potential historic rehabilitation projects, financial tools for preservation-based development, and cultural-heritage program support. In addition, the PDI assessment team was asked by the city to review the use of tax increment financing (TIF) as a way of stimulating growth and to recommend how TIF could be used to the greatest benefit.

In the five years since the PDI, a Main Street program has been established downtown, there has been a market analysis of the downtown district focusing on

Below: *Historic and conservation districts in Pontiac, Michigan.*

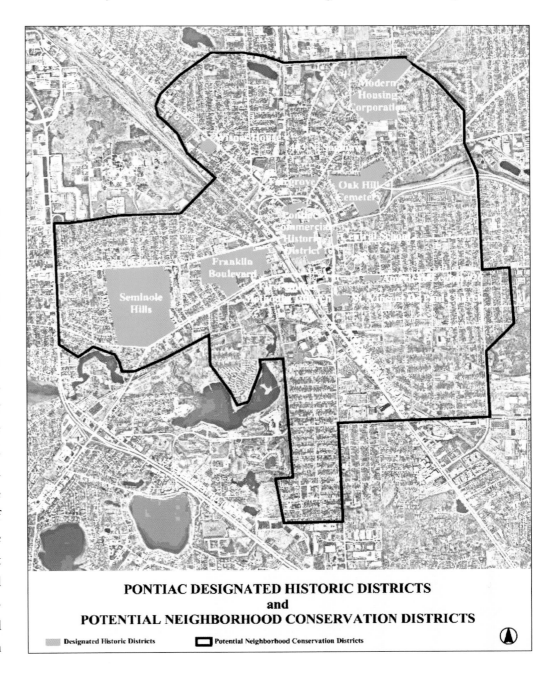

PONTIAC DESIGNATED HISTORIC DISTRICTS
and
POTENTIAL NEIGHBORHOOD CONSERVATION DISTRICTS

Designated Historic Districts   Potential Neighborhood Conservation Districts

Above: *Pontiac in better days: 1941 greeting card.*

percentage of costs that can be taken as a credit is 10 percent for buildings placed in service before 1936, and 20 percent for certified historic structures. From 2001 to 2006, the MHPN estimated, each dollar of tax credit issued by the state brought in more than eleven dollars—adding $2 billion to Michigan's economy.[9]

Conclusions

Urban areas are built on the foundations of long-established communities that have met a wide range of human needs over time. The economic decline of many industrial cities in the Global North has led to degeneration and social deprivation. In the past the solution was to sweep away the rundown areas and start anew, but it is now recognized that renewal is far more sustainable—for people, communities, and the environment. Where investment has taken place within a carefully planned and evaluated program, housing can be improved to meet modern social needs and reach the strict energy targets required to meet the challenges of climate change—and thus be sustainable in social, economic, and environmental terms. Our historic and heritage structures are key to regeneration, and must be renewed to provide the basic needs of warmth, shelter, and security that underpin other human needs.

seven "deal-ready" properties that were able to attract financing and could serve as focal points for additional investment. There have been seminars for developers whose projects could qualify for historic and/or New Markets Tax Credits, which allow taxpayers to claim credit against federal income taxes for investments in entities that invest in low-income neighborhoods, and workshops in "practical preservation" for Pontiac officials and homeowners. There has also been a feasibility study for converting what is called the Standard Vehicle Building into housing, and a design charette for a vacant seven-acre lot owned by the city in the middle of the downtown area, with the intent of evaluating development schemes with a range of stakeholders.

The Michigan Heritage Preservation Network (MHPN) reported that the use of rehabilitation tax credits, which can be applied to costs incurred during the rehabilitation and reconstruction of certain buildings, had been very successful in leveraging further investment from the private sector. (Rehabilitation in this case includes renovation, restoration, and reconstruction but not enlargement or new construction.) Generally, the

Suggested Reading

Luigi Fusco Girard, "Innovative Strategies for Urban Heritage Conservation, Sustainable Development, and Renewable Energy," *Global Urban Development Magazine*, 2 (1), March 2006.

Power of Place: The Future of the Historic Environment. English Heritage, 2000.

Frances Plimmer, Gaye Pottinger, Sarah Harris, Michael Waters, and Yasmin Pocock, *Knock It Down or Do It Up? Sustainable Housebuilding: New Build and Refurbishment in the Sustainable Communities Plan*, BRE Trust Report FB16. Bracknell: IHS BRE Press, 2008.

Tim Yates, *Sustainable Refurbishment of Victorian Housing*, BRE Trust Report FB14. Bracknell, U.K.: IHS BRE Press, 2006.

Notes to Chapter 7

[1] G. Bramley and H. Pawson, "Low Demand for Housing: Incidence, Causes and U.S. National Policy Implications," *Urban Studies* 39(3), 2002, pp. 393–422.

[2] P. Keenan, S. Lowe, and S. Spencer, "Housing Abandonment in Inner Cities—The Politics of Low Demand for Housing," *Housing Studies* 14(5), 1999, pp. 703–16.

[3] Ibid.

[4] A. H. Maslow, "A Theory of Human Motivation," *Psychological Review* 50, 1943, pp. 370–96.

[5] Office of the Deputy Prime Minister, "Sustainable Communities: Building for the Future," 2003.

[6] International Council on Monuments and Sites, "Charter on the Built Vernacular Heritage" (Paris: ICOMOS, 1999).

[7] M. Garb, "If You're Thinking of Living in West Central Harlem; Abandonment Down, Refurbishment Up," *New York Times*, June 21, 1998.

[8] Pontiac Development Initiative, *http://www.nationaltrust.org/community/pontiac_pdi_final.pdf*

[9] Michigan Heritage Preservation Network, "Report Card: The Economic Impacts of Historic Preservation in Michigan," November 2006.

Environmental Priorities and Traditional Ways of Building

Prof. Norman Crowe

> *"Traditional ways of designing provide examples of how everything in a work of architecture may be related to everything else."*

More often than not a building designed to meet high standards of sustainable or "green building" design presents itself as a high-tech machine, conceived in the abstract without a hint of cultural or historical reference to city and community. It is as though 1950s' modernist expressionism had returned to bestow a new focus on architects who had run out of ways to provide an up-to-date technological expression for their designs. While this sort of exercise may be part of an effective approach to basic research and development in green-building technology, such buildings necessarily short-circuit what has historically been meant by the term *architecture*. The alternative, of course, would be to base environmentally sensitive design on tradition. But for many architects steeped in modernist and avant-gardist thinking, traditional design lacks the necessary unique expressive potential to reflect the designer's prowess in green-building technology.

Developing sustainable technologies by means of traditional idioms, however, can provide a truly inclusive basis for design. Arguments against traditional design are many, although for the most part they stem from the linear thinking that characterized early modernism. One argument contends that today's thrust toward economic and cultural globalization renders traditional societies and traditional practices essentially moot—that is to say, we have embarked upon a Brave New World and the eventual fallout can only be guessed. Yet the built environments of traditional societies have evolved over thousands of years through incremental change based on enduring patterns of life and ways of building. Invention was, much like biological transformations, an evolutionary process in which failure was small and corrections made easily, resulting in a kind of perfection of the moment, always open to the next innovation (see page 128).[1]

The importance of shifting architecture, urbanism, and the construction industry toward more sustainable practices is something we can all agree upon. In light of contradictions between narrowly focused environmental determinants and broader, distinctly long-term and overarching environmental and cultural factors, it is clear that the time has come to initiate a broader perspective. It is a problem of mind-set—that is, to establish an ethos that places broader considerations of sustainability as integral to all of the issues that underlie design. Traditional architecture and urbanism can provide both a model and a means for environmentally sensitive design, helping to avoid the problem of jettisoning other important design criteria because of too narrow a focus on specific environment-related determinants. Traditional ways of designing provide examples of how everything in a work of architecture may be related to everything else—often in very subtle ways—where

©ralphrichter/archenova

Left and Below: *Two nontraditional green building designs: a German civic building and an American house. Although touted as highly efficient in heating and cooling, such designs typically preclude regional or other cultural references and disregard embodied energy in the materials of which they are built.*

Right: *Easter Island.*
Once covered by forests, it is
believed that Easter Islanders
eventually denuded their
landscape, leading to their
complete disappearance and
giving rise to the expression
"Easter Island Effect."

architecture and urbanism are seen as interconnected ideas and realities, and where everything is integral to everything else, including the relationship of the building to the natural environment, which makes its existence and ours possible in the first place.

Relating Past and Present Priorities

Part of gaining a better perspective on how we build today is to see ourselves in relation to the past. For instance, if we were to graph the consumption of energy and materials used in the process of building cities, say from the beginning of the Bronze Age to the present, it would reveal a gradual rise throughout history that more or less parallels the growth of human population. It would show that energy resources and the volume of raw materials employed in building settlements remained more or less constant across the ages, albeit with some fluctuation, increasing on the whole only slightly faster than the growth of cities and population throughout the world in response to a gradual increase in the complexity of societies and their economies, and therefore in the average size of buildings and their number in relation to population densities.

Now, if we fast-forward to the beginning of the Industrial Revolution, we see a discernable jump in the graph as new industrialized materials and construction methods are introduced. Then, by the early twentieth century, there is an even more distinct and emphatic upswing. This reflects the use of new, highly processed materials, including metals such as iron and steel, and eventually, aluminum, titanium, synthesized sealants and surfaces, and all the products of modern chemistry now applied to the building industry—including synthesized compounds that are often toxic and virtually unrecyclable. The steep rise of the graph would also reflect a growing reduction in urban densities and the consequent sprawl that necessitates a more elaborate urban infrastructure, including transportation networks to service spread-out

and far-flung destinations for commerce, industry, and living. Moreover, in addition to highly processed or synthesized materials and a changing settlement pattern across the land, our graph would begin to reflect the incorporation of elaborate mechanical systems in buildings, especially central heating and air cooling—mechanisms that permit structures to be built with walls of glass, in which one need only turn up the air-conditioning to compensate for solar gain in summer or turn up the furnace to meet the demands of comfort in the midst of a northern winter. Until recent years, energy was cheap—at least in terms of its immediate up-front costs—and it was thought of as virtually limitless.[2]

Now that we have begun to recognize that the energy sources we rely on most are indeed finite, we have begun to develop new technologies that we trust will eventually return us to that state we call a "sustainable environment." Still, in the rush to find technological solutions to the latest problems caused by technology, we frequently find ourselves standing too close to what we have been doing to see what is happening. Having realized that we must make buildings that are more efficient in their consumption of energy and materials, as well as more sustainable in the overall scheme of things, we almost instinctively turn to the task of engineering an efficient machine of a building, one composed of the latest materials and newest gadgets that state-of-the-art technology can provide. But in doing so—at least if we pursue the problem in such a myopic way—we inevitably surrender subtle characteristics of building long integral to both the culture of building and the culture of the societies the built environment is intended to serve. These "subtle characteristics of building" are found "in the very heart and soul of traditional architecture" as C. W. Westfall has noted. He points out that traditional ways of building are guided by "the conventions that transmit ways of doing things.

" Where architecture and urbanism are seen as interconnected ideas and realities, and where everything is integral to everything else, including the relationship of the building to the natural environment, which makes its existence and ours possible in the first place. "

Conventions, which are among tradition's richest gifts, carry the distilled experience of generations who have successfully solved recurring problems." It is a modern habit of thinking—a prevalent paradigm of our times that emphasizes a stridently linear logic—to isolate a particular problem and solve it to the exclusion of nearly all else, thereby overlooking those conventions "which are among tradition's richest gifts."[3] While isolating a problem to the exclusion of all else is a very efficient way to work, it tends to address only specific fragments of the overall problem. As writers for the Worldwatch Institute have put it:

> Though modern buildings have made living easier for millions, they have also resulted in more subjective problems. Traditionally, local materials and the demands of climate tended to give each indigenous architecture a distinctive character. What shapes modern buildings are the abstract theories of academic architects, the careful calculations of corporations and developers, and the short-run economics of the highly competitive building industry. The result everywhere has been monotonous business and commercial neighborhoods mixed with garish commercial strips. These buildings rarely offer visitors a sense of connection to the fabric of a place, or, by extension, to a community. . . . If the aesthetic freedom granted by industrial materials and fuels carries with it a certain responsibility, then designers and builders have often been derelict in their duties—not just to the natural ecosystems from which life is drawn, but to the people who live and work in their creations.[4]

Traditional architecture, having evolved "naturally"— that is, step-by-step through a process of incremental

" What shapes modern buildings are the abstract theories of academic architects, the careful calculations of corporations and developers, and the short-run economics of the highly competitive building industry. "

Left: *Until recent years energy was cheap and seemed virtually limitless, as the nighttime energy expenditure visible here shows.*

Right: *North America at night, showing the change in illumination 1993–2003. This data is based on satellite observations. Lights are color coded. Red lights appeared during this period. Orange and yellow areas are regions of high- and low-intensity lighting, respectively, which increased in brightness over the ten years. Gray areas are unchanged. Pale blue and dark blue areas are of low- and high-intensity lighting that decreased in brightness. Very dark blue areas were present in 1993 and had disappeared by 2003.*
The U.S. and Canada show increases in brightness, and Mexico shows many new lights, reflecting its urbanization.

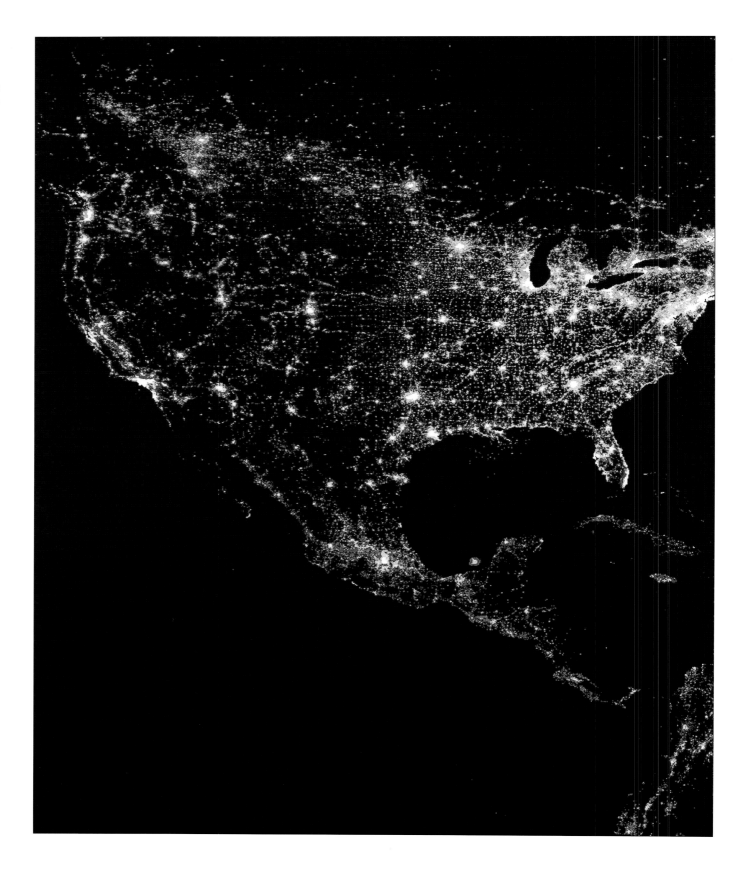

Tehran—are obviously *not* traditional because they are *not* products of long-evolved traditions of the culture in which they stand, nor are they even necessarily attuned to the climatic and topographic conditions of the region in which they are located. Industrial artifacts such as cell-phone relay towers, and most industrial artifacts on the scale of a building—which tend to be virtually the same no matter where we find them—are not traditional by the definition used here, regardless of whether they are new or old or the product of conscious modernist design theory or simply the result of unselfconscious practical engineering. Their forms are often necessary to their functions and they do not pretend to be anything else.

Traditional buildings and traditional urban settings, in the words of early-twentieth-century American architect John Gaw Meem are "elements of our culture that belong to us and help differentiate us." They may be related to an architectural expression that descended from ancient architecture, such as Western classical architecture that has been modified and innovated upon with subtlety over centuries or millennia. Or, at least in some instances, they may be essentially new—modern buildings that have been consciously designed to reflect long-held traditions of the community in whose midst they are intended to reside.

It is indeed a rootedness that traditional forms impart. From a phenomenological perspective, traditional forms are said to help establish a people's sense of "being in the world." In particular, the traditionalness of a setting establishes a people's sense of being an integral part of something larger—perhaps a certain society or culture or city or neighborhood or some combination, or all of these. According to Jane M. Jacobs, geographer at the University of Edinburgh, in the pre-modern world, reliant as it was on tradition, "It is assumed that there was a 'natural' relationship between everyday-lived culture and geographical territory or place—a pre-given or natural order of things embedded in, and confirmed by,

one's locality. . . . Modernity . . . delivers us away from this embedded mode of dwelling, and injects us into a more disembedded and rationalized and individuated being in the world. . . . No longer subjects of fate, we are active agents of rational choice." According to modernist theory, once delivered from the impress of tradition by such forces as globalization, "authority no longer lies outside us, but within us."[8] Modernists saw this as liberation from the tyranny of the past. From the traditionalist perspective, relinquishing the authority of the past places us at the mercy of the unpredictable whims of individual designers and the power structures of today's economies.

With the spread of economic globalization, traditionalism and modernism are now more than ever in conflict for dominance. While modernism and modernist theories have the power to eradicate tradition and thereby diminish traditional cultural identity, they need not do so if a society is sufficiently unified in its desire to sustain itself. Concepts such as "appropriate technologies" attempt to accept and reject technological innovation, economic advances, and cultural forces of external origin, as they are seen to be appropriate or inappropriate to the sustainability of the society and the environment on which that society depends in the long term. But the external forces of economic globalization are strong indeed: selective resistance inevitably meets with effective opposition and generates social acrimony and, ultimately, political strife.

With respect to understanding tradition, it is important to recognize that artifacts of a *living* tradition are necessarily hybrids. In other words, if something is created as part of a living tradition—for instance, a newly constructed building, the establishment of a new settlement or the extension of an existing one, or the creation of a work of art or a useful or beautiful thing of any sort—while it is derived from existing models or paradigms, it is at the same time necessarily different

"*From a phenomenological perspective, traditional forms are said to help establish a people's sense of "being in the world." In particular, the traditionalness of a setting establishes a people's sense of being an integral part of something larger.*"

Opposite and Left:
Del Mar Station, Pasedena, is a development by architects Moule & Polyzoides surrounding one of the most prominent Metro Rail stops connecting Los Angeles and Old Town Pasadena. Co-founders of the Congress for the New Urbanism, a national organization dedicated to reconstructing the American metropolis and preserving natural resources, Moule & Polyzoides also co-wrote the Ahwahnee Principles, a set of community-planning guidelines for the State of California. These principles promote the imperative of linking community with sustainability in town-making and architecture; the importance of regional building traditions; consideration of existing urban settings; respect for the functional and spiritual purposes of architecture; and sensitivity to place and fragility of natural ecosystems.

or Beijing, or comparable portions of New York City, San Francisco, Toronto, or Boston. The difference between the traditional relationship of buildings to streets and squares, and the consequent quality of a public domain that fosters community, as opposed to an exclusively vehicular-oriented pattern—one that prohibits casual interaction among citizens outside the privacy of individual buildings—should be obvious.

Cities pictured here were selected for comparison because they provide a contrast that is sufficiently exaggerated to emphasize the point. More subtle differences are more common, of course. Still, the fundamental principles remain true. The Congress for the New Urbanism, smart growth, and similar contemporary urban reform movements have set as their goal to effect the sort of changes in urban-planning law, development practices, and approaches to design that reinstate important characteristics of traditional urbanism—characteristics that got lost in the translation from pre-industrial paradigms to those of the modernist-inspired, post-industrial present. Traditional architecture, like traditional urbanism, came about under conditions of stringent constraints on the materials available for construction and the energy necessary to ensure human comfort within.

Traditional Architecture and Environmental Priorities

A list of the more noteworthy architects of the twentieth century whose work springs directly from traditional forms and who emphasize environmental priorities, would include Hasan Fathy of Egypt, Charles Correa of India, Sedad Hakki Eldem of Turkey, Dimitri Pikionis of Greece, John Gaw Meem of New Mexico, Elizabeth Moule and Stefanos Polyzoides of Los Angeles, and Wu Liangyung of China. This is a shortlist; there are many more. In the parlance of architectural historians, each of

" No other art feels its influence so decisively . . . the prevailing technology changes every few decades. And each time this happens, architecture must reinvent the expression of the mythic images and values on which it is based. "

these architects is referred to as a "regionalist." Each has responded to ongoing architectural traditions that recognize specific characteristics of climate: Egypt's relentless desert heat; South India's tropical humidity and seasonal monsoons; Turkey's and Greece's hot, dry summers tempered by cool nights; New Mexico's hot, dry summers and cold winter nights; and so forth.

A look at a few examples demonstrates the point. India's Correa, for instance, asserts that the forces that shape his architecture may be found "at the deep structural level, climatic conditions, culture and its expression, its rites and ritual. In itself, climate is the source of myth: thus the metaphysical quantities attributed to open-to-the-sky space in the cultures of India . . . are concomitants of the warm climate in which they exist." Regarding the force of technology, he points out that "No other art feels its influence so decisively . . . the prevailing technology changes every few decades. And each time this happens, architecture must reinvent the expression of the mythic images and values on which it is based."[9] Judging by the evidence of his existing work, "reinvention" did not mean starting from scratch, but rather starting from a firm basis in well-established traditional ways of building, utilizing for the most part familiar, traditional materials. Correa's words reveal that it is a frame of mind that animates the relationship between tradition and invention—and the mythological as well as the rational, the imaginary as much as the real—as revealed in his Belapur Housing.

Hasan Fathy reinterpreted the traditional Egyptian home to adapt it to more contemporary ways of living, while employing natural cooling and ventilation techniques found in traditional buildings that utilized natural gravity circulation and evaporative cooling (see page 144). He employed materials of low embodied energy such as stone and mud brick, depending on local sources and traditionally trained craftsmen.

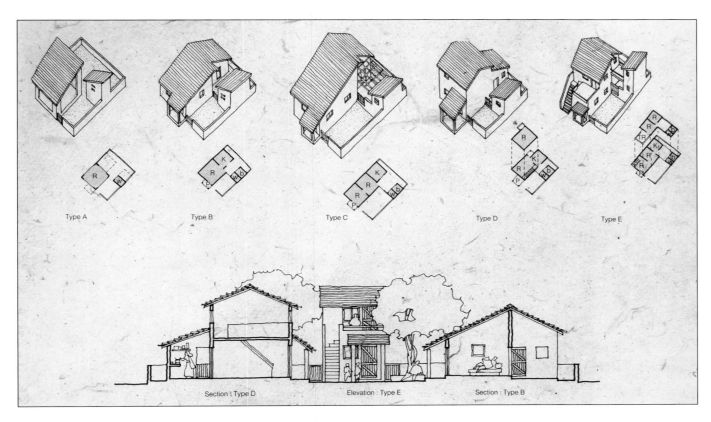

Type A   Type B   Type C   Type D   Type E

Section : Type D   Elevation : Type E   Section : Type B

Figure 1: *Housing by architect Charles Correa in Belapur, New Bombay, India, 1983–86. The housing types provide for expansion and expression of individuality for each family.*

Left: *Correa's housing in Belapur incorporates the traditional South Indian idea of the courtyard.*

Figure 2: *Hamdi Seif al-Nasr Resthouse, Fayyum, Egypt, preliminary design, 1944, by architect Hassan Fathy. A wind catcher on the side of the dome directs a current of dry desert air down over a plate, wet from a trickle of water from an overhanging vessel. The air, cooled by evaporation, drops further and passes into the domed main hall. As the air rewarms, it rises up and out of the openings in the dome.*

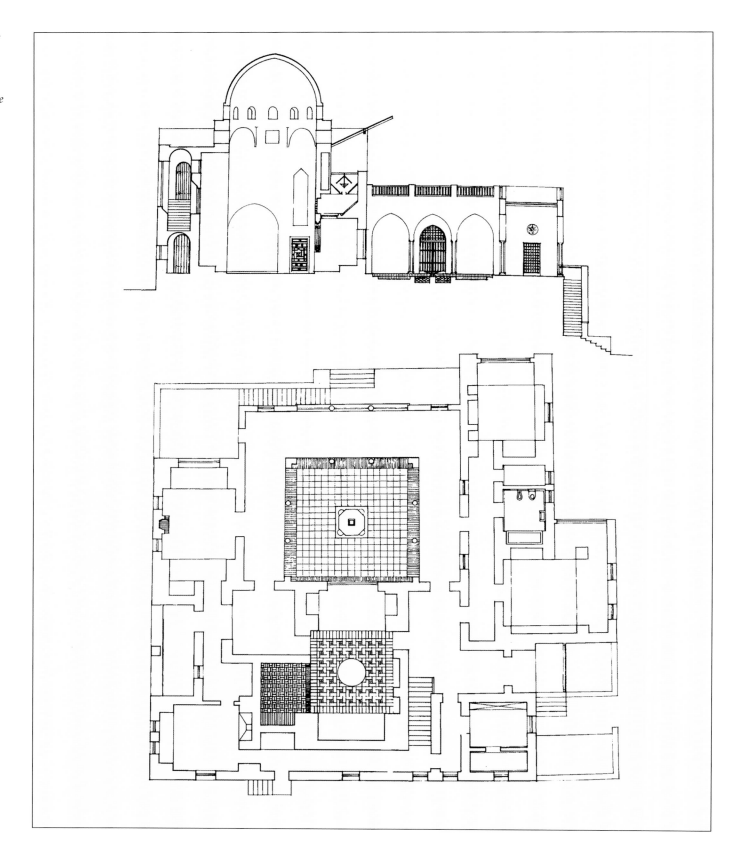

In antiquity, *virtù* meant "excellence" and "good action," with an emphasis on the latter. The ancient Roman writer and orator M. Tullius Cicero described the civic virtues and their division into discrete parts in his *De inventione* from the first century B.C.[9] He defined virtue as a "habit of mind in harmony with reason and the order of nature," and divided it into four parts: Prudence, Justice, Fortitude, and Temperance. Cicero classified memory (*memoria*) along with intelligence (*intelligentia*) and foresight (*providentia*) as the constituent elements of Prudence.[10] The three components would ensure that the prudent individual would know "what has happened," "what is," and "what is going to occur before it occurs." Prudence was a behavioral guide, an anticipatory inner vision gained from experience, that when applied to building allowed the architect to look well into the future with tremendous authority.

One of the most important sixteenth-century Italian humanists to write on virtue was Alvise (Luigi) Cornaro, an Italian nobleman born in the late fifteenth century who at the age of eighty-three wrote his *Discorsi intorno alla vita sobria* (1558), a eulogy of moderation and leisure that proclaimed the joys of health and longevity.[11] Cornaro was born in Venice between 1475 and 1484. He moved to Padua after having inherited his uncle's estate there, and became a leading figure in the city's humanist circle. He dedicated his life to balancing the activities of landowner with interests in literature and architecture. Yet Cornaro's early life was typical for a man of his noble status—he indulged in food and wine quite liberally until he reached middle age. Approaching the winter of his life and unhappy with his constitution, Cornaro consulted his physician, who advised the only course available to him was to reform his habits of eating and drinking. Cornaro was so impressed that he devoted the remainder of his life to the diligent pursuit of moderation, for, in his delightful words, such an approach to life:

Left: *Statue of Leon Battista Alberti in the Uffizi Gallery, Florence.*

renders the senses clear, the body light, the understanding lively, the soul brisk, the memory tenacious, our motions free, and all our actions regular and easy . . . the soul . . . experiences a great deal of her natural liberty; the spirits circulate gently through the arteries; the blood runs freely through the veins; the heat of the body, kept mild

Below and Opposite: *Alvise Cornaro's home in Padua contained the first all'antica buildings in the Veneto: the Loggia (**Below**) and Odeon Cornaro (**Opposite**), built by Giovanni Maria Falconetto about 1524.*

and temperate, has mild and temperate effects; and, lastly, our faculties, being under a perfect regulation, preserve a pleasing and agreeable harmony.[12]

Alvise Cornaro lived to be over eighty years of age, proclaiming how those who knew him would testify to the good state of health and spirits he enjoyed. Yet his account of *virtù* was more than a simple memoir. It was a call to those who believed that life after sixty was a living death to come and visit him, and see firsthand how moderation could improve the quality of one's life. If Cicero's account of the virtues and their parts played an important role in the formulation of the four cardinal virtues, then Cornaro's writings were instrumental in passing on to posterity the idea that architecture is a kind

technical difficulties associated with irrigation and land yield, problems that inspired Palladio to design a machine for "raising the water from low-lying places."[23] It is not surprising to find that Cornaro's pamphlet begins with a eulogy of the *vita sobria*, and the benefits that such an attitude conveys to all aspects of life.

Creativity

The sixteenth-century Veneto witnessed a remarkable social program of architecture and landscape that was rooted in virtue and excellence. This moral imperative was not simply expressed in noble palaces and public buildings, but also extended to the habitations of all sectors of society. Artistic creativity was the vehicle for carrying out such a program, and perhaps no one set the pace faster than Sebastiano Serlio, whose books on architecture were decidedly didactic and aimed at improving the knowledge of architecture's role in shaping the built environment. Fundamental to Serlio's success was the wealth of practical solutions he provided to the problem of how to apply classical architecture to contemporary needs. As the title of his Sixth Book, *Of Habitations Suitable for all Grades of Men*, suggests, Serlio set out to produce a comprehensive anthology of residential building types covering the entire social spectrum.[24] The book deals with both urban and rural residences, treating princely palaces and middle-class buildings accordingly. More important, he provides the reader with a clear set of guiding principles (mostly plans and elevations) for the design and construction of bourgeois architecture, an idea that was gaining ground in the Veneto in the middle half of the sixteenth century.

Serlio provided stylistic parallels of residential types based on a classification that varied between five and seven social classes. Though the distinction between the classes is often hazy, the stylistic parallel is clear: an Italianate building is contrasted with a regional alternative, usually French, or Dutch. As far as typological variation is concerned, the more utilitarian or primitive the structure, the less architectural innovation is provided. In the case of more sophisticated and aristocratic residences, great expense is afforded to variations in plan, elevation, decoration, and style. Not surprisingly, the bulk of noble residences are invariably classical and Italianate. Where background urban fabric is concerned, regional character and established building traditions are essential. In the case of noble residences, the universal aspects of order and decorum play a far more important role, guiding the character and conduct of the building in relation to the larger urban structure, an idea previously formulated by Alberti but never given light until now.

Serlio reveals further evidence of Alberti's influence in his attitude that a building can be beautiful and

Left: *Sebastiano Serlio's (1475–1554) books on architecture were aimed at improving the knowledge of architecture's role in shaping the built environment. This is a proposal for the Odeon Cornaro from his seventh book.*

161

employ neither Doric nor Ionic nor Corinthian columns.[25] In describing the advantage, or disadvantage, of custom, Alberti wrote, "[O]ther famous architects seem to recommend by their work either the Doric, or the Ionic, or the Corinthian, or the Tuscan division as being the most convenient, there is no reason why we should follow their design in our work, as though legally obliged; but rather, inspired by their example, we should strive to produce our own inventions, to rival, or, if possible, to surpass the glory of theirs." Alvise Cornaro echoed Alberti's attitude toward canonical classicism in his manuscript treatise on architecture, and also considered the question of popular housing, though he provided no such graphic information as to how to design for it. In any event, Serlio had frequented Cornaro's academy in Padua and subsequently illustrated

Below: *A beautiful double-page spread from Sebastiano Serlio's fourth book.*

his master's house in Padua, the Odeon Cornaro, with a steeply pitched roof and French-style Mannerist dormers, presumably as creative license and a suggestion to his mentor as to how he might improve the original structure.[26] Finally, it is worth noting that Book VII, which deals with accidents and unusual situations in building, covers a topic that was curiously novel at the time and extremely relevant to Serlio's domestic schemes: how to restore and renovate older buildings to suit modern needs—an idea that is fundamental to the current green movement.

Serlio's books on architecture were in many ways a plea to the architectural virtues of common sense and humility when dealing with residential architecture, particularly where *all'antica* architecture was concerned. But this does not suggest that the classical orders were purely optional ingredients determined by taste. It would be misleading to think that Serlio reduced the entire theory of the orders to a catalogue of decorative details. Rather, his concern with bourgeois dwellings was a profound recognition of the value of vernacular building and its implicit relationship with the language of classical architecture. The two are inseparable, not antithetical, and in this way Serlio is positing a middle approach to classical invention, one that seeks a temperate balance between grandeur and starvation.

The Recovery of Tradition

Gian Giorgio Trissino was an Italian nobleman, diplomat, and scholar who had met Alvise Cornaro while in Padua from 1538 to 1540. Their relationship must have solidified quickly, for the two men shared a profound interest in the humanist debates of the time. From approximately 1536 on, Trissino was engaged in the rebuilding of his villa at Cricoli, near Vicenza, (see photograph on page 164) in order to create an academy along the lines of Lorenzo de' Medici's in Florence. It was

Left: *Portrait of Gian Giorgio Trissino by Vincenzo Catena.*

there that Trissino came into contact with a young stone mason, Andrea di Pietro della Gondola, upon whom he later bestowed the name Palladio. The name refers to a unique character from an epic poem that Trissino had published in 1547, *L'Italia liberata dai Goti* (Italy liberated from the Goths). The poem recounted the legendary tale of Emperor Justinian's liberation of Italy in the fifth century. The key figure in the poem was a guardian angel, Palladio, who was sent to earth by God as a guide and helpmate in expelling the Goths from Italy. His expertise in architectural matters enabled Justinian's commander Belisarius to maneuver his way through an enemy-occupied palace, leading his troops to victory. The conferring of the name was doubly allusive insofar as the young mason was not only well versed in architecture but had also displayed a talent that could easily be associated with the image of Pallas Athena.[27] At any rate, Palladio's association with Trissino not only resulted in his change

Above: *Trissino was rebuilding his villa at Cricoli near Vicenza, in order to create an academy along the lines of Lorenzo de' Medici's in Florence when he met Andrea di Pietro della Gondola.*

Opposite: *Palladio's covered wooden pontoon bridge at Bassano, built in 1569 (it has been rebuilt many times since then).*

of profession, but more importantly exposed him to the writings of Vitruvius and the monuments of antiquity, for the two traveled together to Rome from 1545 to 1547. It is generally recognized that Palladio was invited to participate in discussions with Trissino and Cornaro in Padua. Palladio later regarded Cornaro as a "nobleman of excellent judgment," and applied the latter's teachings to his own works.[28] A passage from Palladio's *Four Books on Architecture* reveals the author's tremendous respect for Cornaro's ideas:

[H]ouses in cities really are splendid and convenient for the gentleman, since he has to live in them throughout the period that he needs for the administration of the community and running his own affairs. But he will perhaps find the buildings on his estate no less useful and comforting, where he will pass the rest of the time watching over and improving his property and increasing his wealth through his skill in farming, and where, by means of the exercise that

Right: *San Giorgio Maggiore, Venice, by Palladio.*

one usually takes on the country estate on foot or on horseback, his body will more readily maintain its healthiness and strength, and where, finally, someone whose spirit is tired by the aggravations of the city will be revitalized, soothed, and will be able to attend in tranquility to the study of literature and quiet contemplation; similarly this was why the sensible men of the ancient world made a habit of withdrawing frequently to such places where, visited by brilliant friends and relatives, they could easily pursue that good life which they could enjoy there since they had lodgings, gardens, fountains, and similar soothing locales, and above all their own virtù.[29]

Palladio, of course, is celebrated for much more than his private residences, be they in the city or countryside. When one considers the full repertoire of his work—designs for sacred buildings, meeting halls, bridges, theaters, gates, portals, and machinery—one discovers a breadth of vision and talent that far exceeds his reputation as the world's most influential high-end residential architect. It is perhaps this least recognized aspect of Palladio's career—the role of gifted civic activist—that is most relevant to contemporary practice. For it was in Venice that Palladio received his greatest title as Architectus Illustrissimi Dominii Veneti (Architect of the Most Illustrious Dominion of the Venetians). Unlike his more familiar pseudonym, which spoke of divine inspiration and exceptional talent—what we call genius in architectural circles today—it was in Venice that the respected Andrea di Pietro dalla Gondola was considered the architect of one of the greatest Renaissance cities that Europe has produced.

The idea that architecture fulfilled a major social and ethical function—cultural sustainability—was a

Below: *"La Rotunda" in Vicenza by Palladio.*

Right: *Trissino gave Andrea the name we know him by today—Palladio.*

ANDREA PALLADIO

ARCHITETTO

concern that occupied architects and planners in the early Renaissance, when the modern conception of a humane architecture was first expounded. In describing the suitable habitations for well-being (*benessere*), architects and writers on architecture such as Leon Battista Alberti, Alvise Cornaro, Sebastiano Serlio, Gian Giorgio Trissino, and Palladio focused on the profound importance that common sense, natural systems, memory, and decorum played in shaping the quality and character of buildings, particularly in relation to the larger built environment. The gradation from vernacular building to classical architecture was inseparable from considerations of regional character, affordability, comfort, and established building traditions.

Today, most architects and planners are aware that tradition is a necessary ingredient of cultural sustainability, yet few consider the Renaissance conception of well-being in relation to the design of beautiful and meaningful places. Given the contemporary crises of our cities and towns, and the increasing division between economic levels and age groups, nothing could be more relevant than a good dose of Renaissance sobriety. If cultural sustainability is to become a critical concern of architects, then it is time to reconsider the lessons of sixteenth-century humanist culture as it relates to creating a more humane and sustainable natural and built environment. Only then will discussions of green architecture be truly invaluable.

schemes that optimize sites formerly used by industry or for other purposes.

Reducing Carbon at the Scale of the Building

The sustainability agenda as it relates to the built environment is multifaceted, and in the last five years the Prince's Foundation has taken an active interest in the material science of low-energy building. The challenge, as the Foundation sees it, is to try and achieve a meaningful balance between the carbon cost of sourcing and manufacturing building materials, and the materials'

proven ability to provide passive cooling in summer and heating in winter. Accordingly, the emphasis has been on researching effective methods that satisfy these criteria but can be produced at reasonable cost. The Foundation is taking on this challenge because the market is reluctant to undertake research at its own cost. Moreover, conventional house builders have been historically averse to innovation that would affect their supply chains, which are tuned to deliver significant cost margins.

The carbon debate as it relates to residential construction in the U.K. has largely centered on the

Above: *Prince's Foundation mixed use development at Westoe, Sunderland.*

energy performance of individual homes. A new regulatory framework (the Code for Sustainable Homes) intended to produce a new generation of energy-efficient houses is currently causing significant headaches for house builders in the U.K. The assumption among energy scientists and architects, meanwhile, is that all previous practice in residential building is obsolete.

When the Code for Sustainable Homes was launched in the U.K. in 2006, house builders who had spent years developing homes with popular appeal and finely honed costs were suddenly being challenged to build according to the new low-energy paradigm. At the outset, the code demanded the steady upgrade of existing building regulations for energy performance until homes are "zero carbon," that is, use only energy generated by carbon-free means, by 2016. The exact definition of "zero carbon" remains opaque, and this has led to many false starts on the road to energy efficiency. Wooden "kit" frames that represent carbon-neutral structure, large expanses of glazing that afford "solar gain" to heat buildings, and an array of photovoltaic panels and miniature turbines adorning the roofscape have all, in turn, been urged on the bewildered residential builder trying to minimize carbon impact.

The usefulness of many of these solutions—some of the feeble miniturbines would be hard pressed to light a forty-watt bulb—has been debunked in the course of the fierce dialogue of subsequent years. Many wood-framed houses have a tendency to overheat on warm summer days, as they lack the thermal mass that keeps the sun's energy out of the building. Furthermore, the overriding dependence on technology and the highly complex array of insulating membranes means that many such buildings are out of reach of affordable delivery in the U.K. and, when their complex systems fail, they're doomed to obsolescence. There remains, however, a small but vociferous group of architects who insist that the low-energy home of the future must inevitably be

"The perceived high-maintenance burden of experimental environmental features— such as turbines and photovoltaics, graywater systems and programmed climate control—make them unattractive to a public used to enjoying homes whose selling points are ease of maintenance and operation."

Left: *First-generation low-carbon scheme; BedZED, South London.*

181

different from homes of the past, and that technological change will drive the form of new homes.

The difficulty is that the majority of new homes built in the U.K. have hitherto been copybook designs tailored to the taste of a conservative buying public. Many homeowners are by no means convinced of the merits of a low-energy building, especially when these are presented in their more radical incarnations. The subscribers of early low-carbon builds tend to be the environmentally zealous, whereas those who are indifferent to or ignorant of climate issues tend to choose conventional homes of traditional appearance. The perceived high-maintenance burden of experimental environmental features—such as turbines and photovoltaics, graywater systems and programmed climate control—make them unattractive to a public used to enjoying homes whose selling points are ease of maintenance and operation.

The Prince's Foundation for the Built Environment repudiates the assumption that our most significant twenty-first century problem—global warming—necessitates entirely radical built forms that entirely reject earlier generations of housing. The Foundation's first impulse was to look further back into tradition—if the twentieth century was the era of cheap and plentiful energy, shouldn't we look for lessons on energy conservation to previous epochs in domestic architecture, when energy was not abundant and resources were valued because of their scarcity? Furthermore, the primary concern of any green-building project should be to reduce the energy requirement of the building first and foremost before asking questions about where the energy came from.

Genesis of the Natural House

The Foundation set itself the challenge of designing and building an eco house that took into consideration its

environmental burden in the selection of materials (as low-impact as possible), the longevity of the finished product, and the energy requirements of the building when in use. This meant reducing the need for heating and cooling to the absolute minimum in a building envelope that would be easy to build in a wide variety of conditions. The Foundation also strove for solutions that would be easy for the "lay householder" (who has to live in the building) to understand and easy to maintain in the long term. Further criteria for consideration were that the house should be able to be delivered at reasonable cost, and reflect current standards in site conditions and availability of materials.

"The Natural House" was initiated by the Prince's Foundation for the Built Environment in partnership with the specialist consultancy Natural Building Technologies. It is made of natural materials grown in or taken from the ground. It achieves energy efficiency through simple wall construction of sound thermal mass that can be produced from locally sourced materials and built by local labor. The organization is building and testing this trial house in response to the challenge of the Code for Sustainable Homes and other carbon reduction targets, as this research was not, to our knowledge, being conducted by the mainstream building industry.

BRE Innovation Park

The opportunity to undertake such an ambitious project came with the offer to develop a house for the Building Research Establishment's "Innovation Park," a collection of demonstration houses built by different consortia in the building industry to test a variety of approaches to energy efficiency. The first phase of Innovation Park, conducted between 2005 and 2007, presented a variety of single-home designs of idiosyncratically modern appearance. The projects featured mono-pitch roofs, extensive glazing in asymmetrical patterns, and the

Opposite: *Building Research Establishment's (BRE) Innovation Park.*

Right: *Hemcrete wall built at Lincoln Cathedral by Prince's Foundation building craft apprentices in 2007.*

prominent siting of renewable technologies for symbolic effect. Many of the houses aspired to—and achieved—the highest levels of the Code for Sustainable Homes, including the provision of energy from on-plot resources, although the reliability of these resources was variable. The predominant construction methods focused on offsite manufacture—several of the builds made a virtue out of their rapid construction techniques and went up in a matter of days. Each of these first-generation houses was designed as an isolated composition, paying little heed to other houses on the site or the overall layout.

Despite being strongly endorsed by government, in particular through the promotion of a "Design for Manufacture; £60k House" competition, modern methods of production have proved problematic in market conditions. A design by Richard Rogers, lauded by the competition organizers, was plagued by technical difficulties when 145 examples were built at Oxley Woods, Milton Keynes. Residents have reported repeated problems with water penetration since the houses' completion, raising concerns about the performance of panelized construction methods for walls and glazing.

With offsite manufacture subject to review, the second generation of development in the Park saw BRE take a rather different approach when encouraging new partners. Having considered the benefits and short-comings of offsite construction, BRE was keen to test the possibilities of using materials from natural sources and

U-values (a measure of whether a material allows heat to pass through). Its performance (U values of 0.2) is similar to that of many of the offsite manufacturing processes but offers a simplicity and robustness of construction that ensures performance in the long term. Much of the insulating value is conferred by the trapped air pockets, supported by the external render and internal plaster, all naturally sourced.

Thus, the house contradicts the assumption that high technology will save the day, achieving its energy savings through good thermal mass, sound insulation for floors and roof, triple-glazed windows that afford good natural lighting, and a well-proportioned approach to design with a balanced wall-to-window ratio.

House Typology

The Natural House trumpets the merits of community-based living—fulfilling the core philosophy of the Foundation that a sustainable future for mankind relies upon obtaining the ingredients for city- and town-making in place, so that energy resources are no longer squandered on unnecessary traveling for one's daily needs. The Foundation was therefore keen to show an "urban typology" at the BRE Innovation Park: a house

Figure 2: *Variations on the house design showing two-, three-, and four-story versions of the prototype.*

189

Right: *House under construction, September 2009.*

Below Right: *HRH Prince of Wales visits the construction site.*

Opposite: *Rendering showing final design.*

Figure 3: *Plans showing how the house design conforms to strong block-based urban form.*

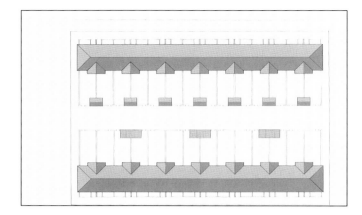 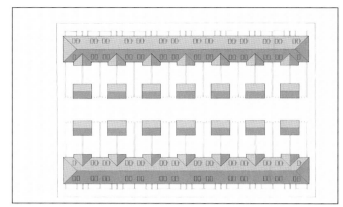

design that could be suitably adapted to a semi-detached configuration or rolled out as a terrace house. Alternative layouts with two, three, and four stories have also been considered in detail. The aim is to demonstrate that high-quality residential design is possible even when building for higher densities, reflecting patterns visible throughout our Victorian and Edwardian suburbs.

The Foundation also noticed the trend in these suburbs toward "pairing" houses by devices such as pediments or recessed doorways, so that even when houses are terraced they read as independent dwellings in the tradition of the English country house. After all, inside every suburban homeowner there lurks a nascent country gentleman or gentlewoman.

The house is designed, of course, for mass replication without falling into the trap of monotonous repetition. A series of variations are envisaged, all sharing a basic common-plan type but showing an adaptive variety. The capacity for adaptation extends to anticipating changing needs over time; the house can be a family home, subdivided into flats, or adapted for other uses, all without compromising the basic thermal envelope.

In the house designed for BRE, a three-bedroom family home is paired with a small ground-floor studio and a first-floor maisonette, which utilizes the insulated roof space for bedrooms. Any of these elements is interchangeable in subsequent iterations of the house.

For purposes of clarity, the side walls have been left without windows (the chimney stacks occupying part of the area) to demonstrate how well the plan would work in terraced configuration.

Building work commenced in the spring of 2009, with completion scheduled for the end of the year. However, the end of the construction phase marks only the start of the most critical phase of the project, in which the house will be tested as part of the national strategy for the implementation of the Code for Sustainable Homes. A second generation of pilots at the Foundation's Coed-Darcy development in South Wales is already in the planning stages. Interest in the project continues to grow.

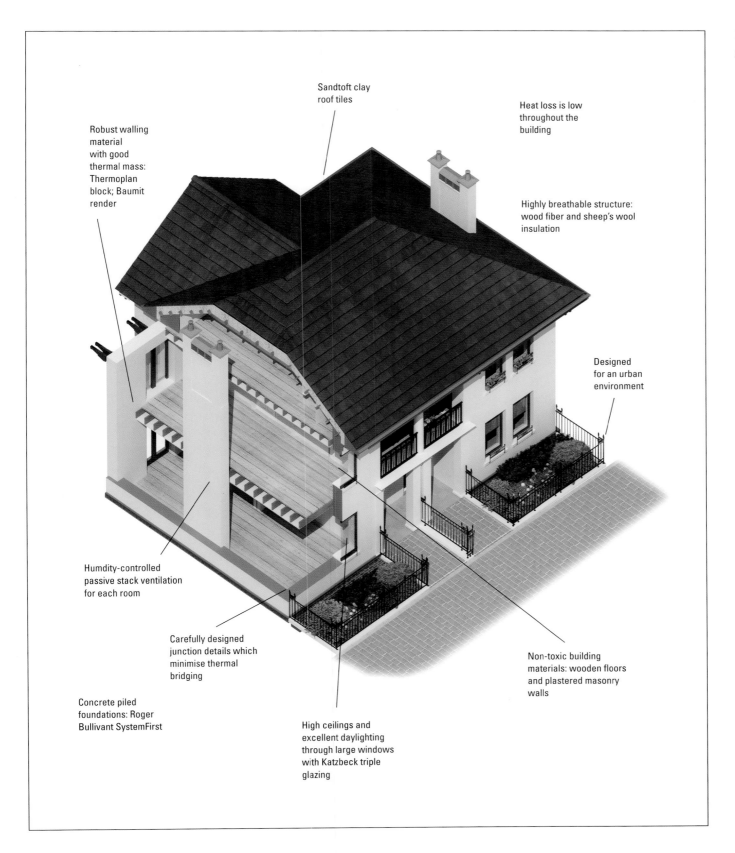

Figure 4: *Cut away showing principal building components.*

Sandtoft clay roof tiles

Heat loss is low throughout the building

Robust walling material with good thermal mass: Thermoplan block; Baumit render

Highly breathable structure: wood fiber and sheep's wool insulation

Designed for an urban environment

Humdity-controlled passive stack ventilation for each room

Carefully designed junction details which minimise thermal bridging

Non-toxic building materials: wooden floors and plastered masonry walls

Concrete piled foundations: Roger Bullivant SystemFirst

High ceilings and excellent daylighting through large windows with Katzbeck triple glazing

193

The Green Tradition:

Innovating the Future

Dr. Barbara Kenda

We now know what we need to do. We need to reduce greenhouse gas emissions and our dependence on oil. We need to move away from the outdated fossil-fuel economy, from coal-fired utilities, from mercury emissions that are causing global climate change, hazardous air pollution, and damage to our health. We know that we need to reduce the consumption of materials used to make buildings, and the consumption of energy resources by completed buildings.

The negative impact of the building industry on the environment has been tremendous. The Worldwatch Institute has estimated that "one-tenth of the global economy is dedicated to constructing and operating buildings; buildings consume one-sixth to one-half of the world's resources; the building industry uses . . . about forty percent of all materials entering the global market annually; approximately thirty percent of greenhouse gas emissions in the U.S. come from buildings, and buildings consume sixty-two percent of the total electrical use in the U.S."[1]

Modern buildings are often guided by the abstract theories of academic architects and urbanists that nobody understands. Such architecture of ephemeral fashions cannot survive. Far too often, modern buildings are shaped by a highly competitive building industry, unsustainable materials, short-run economics, and the myopic visions of developers and governmental planners, resulting in increased greenhouse gas emissions, air pollution, monotonous business and commercial neighborhoods or nonwalkable suburban residential sprawl. Such places, in the opinion of the Worldwatch Institute, "rarely offer visitors a sense of connection to the fabric of a place, or, by extension, to a community. . . . If the aesthetic freedom granted by industrial materials

Right: *Al Gore, the founder and chair of the Alliance for Climate Protection.*

and fuels carries with it a certain responsibility, then designers and builders have often been derelict in their duties—not just in their ecosystems from which life is drawn, but to the people who live and work in their creations."[2]

Sustainable design is increasingly shaping this century's architecture and planning. But do all green architects today understand the meaningful relationship between a building's structure, function, art, and nature? Many contemporary architects build their work on the proposition that sustainability may be achieved using

nothing more than better materials and mechanical gizmos.[3] Their designs refute any reference to the past, to the embodied energy of materials, or to greenhouse gas emissions. Consequently, much of contemporary architecture continues to disregard environmental, regional, and cultural identity, and thus fails to attain architectural and urban beauty. "The secret of avant-garde architecture is that it's easy to invent new shapes. Children do it all the time. . . . What's hard is to give those shapes and forms any meaning. You can't do that without referring to some kind of tradition."[4]

Opposite: *Earthship home, Taos, New Mexico. Earthship buildings are a type of passive solar home, made of natural and recycled materials. They are built to minimize environmental impact and to use local resources, such as sunlight. Solar panels are used to generate electricity; glass windows, to trap warmth. The first Earthship homes were designed in the 1970s by Mike Reynolds, founder of Earthship Biotecture.*

Above Left: *The Lyle Center for Regenerative Studies at California State Polytechnic University, Pomona. The buildings at the center are designed to minimize the amount of energy required for heating and cooling. Here a trellis structure on the south side of the building supports grapes, chayote, and other deciduous vines. The shade from the vines blocks direct sunlight from entering the building in the summer. In the winter, the vines lose their leaves and lower sun angles allow direct sunlight to penetrate into the interior spaces, passively warming the building. Also visible but inconspicuous are four solar heater panels on the roof. A recycling garbage bin is seen in front of the building. Photo December 2008.*

Left: *Straw bale house by Athena Steen.*

Right: *Traditional Swiss architecture. Timber-frame wall with the gaps filled with clay and large gravel stones. This is an example of the traditional architecture of Swiss towns, where local wood and stones were used in the building of houses. This is part of the wall of the old mill in the town of Marthalen, Switzerland.*

Our purpose here is not so much to reiterate our concerns and our duties as to explore the question of how we should build.[5] How can we abandon our bad habits and use our collective intelligence to create a healthy post-industrial future? How do we move toward renewable energy sources and increase the energy efficiency of buildings? And how do we build attractive environments? This book argues for ethical solutions and presents innovative examples of built environment through the lens of the original green.

Traditional architects and urbanists of the past few decades have relied on original green. They "innovate on the edge of tradition." They use naturally built environments of past cultures as models for sound planning and building because they are beautiful, sustainable, humane, and timeless and because they promote the art of well-being. Hassan Fathy, Charles Correa, John Gaw Meem, B. H. C. Patel, Abdel-Wahed El-Wakil, Rasem Badran, Dimitri Pikionis, Imre Makovecz, Robert Adam, Léon Krier, and others have fused sustainable and frugal technologies, and natural energy resources, with good design. They innovate with solar and wind power, with geothermal springs, with hemp and straw bale, with local resources, and with powerful natural air-conditioning systems. Paraphrasing traditional languages, forms, and concepts, and invoking cultural and historical dimensions of a place, such designs can help define the future of changing styles and technologies.

The previous essays represent a renaissance of an intuitive cross-cultural wisdom about places. They provide examples of green design aimed at the